W9-AQN-938

DESEGREGATION AND THE SUPREME COURT

Problems in American Civilization

UNDER THE EDITORIAL DIRECTION OF

George Rogers Taylor

PURITANISM IN EARLY AMERICA

THE CAUSES OF THE AMERICAN REVOLUTION

BENJAMIN FRANKLIN AND THE AMERICAN CHARACTER

THE DECLARATION OF INDEPENDENCE AND THE CONSTITUTION

HAMILTON AND THE NATIONAL DEBT

THE TURNER THESIS CONCERNING THE ROLE OF THE FRONTIER IN AMERICAN HISTORY

THE GREAT TARIFF DEBATE, 1820–1830

JACKSON VERSUS BIDDLE – THE STRUGGLE OVER THE SECOND BANK OF THE UNITED STATES

THE TRANSCENDENTALIST REVOLT AGAINST MATERIALISM

THE COMPROMISE OF 1850

SLAVERY AS A CAUSE OF THE CIVIL WAR

RECONSTRUCTION IN THE SOUTH

MARK TWAIN'S *Huckleberry Finn*

DEMOCRACY AND THE GOSPEL OF WEALTH

JOHN D. ROCKEFELLER – ROBBER BARON OR INDUSTRIAL STATESMAN?

THE PULLMAN BOYCOTT OF 1894 – THE PROBLEM OF FEDERAL INTERVENTION

WILLIAM JENNINGS BRYAN AND THE CAMPAIGN OF 1896

AMERICAN IMPERIALISM IN 1898

ROOSEVELT, WILSON, AND THE TRUSTS

PRAGMATISM AND AMERICAN CULTURE

WILSON AT VERSAILLES

THE NEW DEAL – REVOLUTION OR EVOLUTION?

FRANKLIN D. ROOSEVELT AND THE SUPREME COURT

PEARL HARBOR – ROOSEVELT AND THE COMING OF THE WAR

THE YALTA CONFERENCE

INDUSTRY-WIDE COLLECTIVE BARGAINING – PROMISE OR MENACE?

EDUCATION FOR DEMOCRACY – THE DEBATE OVER THE REPORT OF THE PRESIDENT'S COMMISSION ON HIGHER EDUCATION

EVOLUTION AND RELIGION – THE CONFLICT BETWEEN SCIENCE AND THEOLOGY IN MODERN AMERICA

IMMIGRATION – AN AMERICAN DILEMMA

LOYALTY IN A DEMOCRATIC STATE

DESEGREGATION AND THE SUPREME COURT

DESEGREGATION AND THE SUPREME COURT

EDITED WITH AN INTRODUCTION BY

Benjamin Munn Ziegler

Problems in American Civilization

READINGS SELECTED BY THE
DEPARTMENT OF AMERICAN STUDIES
AMHERST COLLEGE

D. C. HEATH AND COMPANY: Boston

PRINTED IN THE UNITED STATES OF AMERICA

INTRODUCTION

ON May 17, 1954, the Supreme Court ruled that "in the field of public education the doctrine of 'separate but equal' has no place. Separate educational facilities are inherently unequal." It is difficult to say whether this decision on segregation in public schools has focused more attention upon the segregation problem itself or upon the proper role of the Supreme Court in our system of government. There is little doubt, however, that both are inextricably connected. In part this may be due to the fact that so volcanic a question has been settled by court decision and that the decision, of necessity, delves deeply into the complex relationship between morality and politics, between historical traditions and present predicaments. But it is due also to the fact that the Courts, particularly the Supreme Court, have occupied a unique position and through it have exercised a unique power in our governmental structure. What we have before us, therefore, is a problem within a problem. It is first a problem of how the Courts have come to fill this position as well as the manner and method in which it has been filled. It is, secondly, an example of the exercise of its power in a particular problem, "Desegregation." And the issues joined come down to this: Should this power, in a democracy like ours, be left to the Courts, and has it, in the immediate question before us, been exercised in accord with our Constitutional principles?

In No. 51 of *The Federalist* James Madison wrote that "in framing a government which is to be administered by men over men, the great difficulty lies in this: you must first enable the Government to control the governed; and in the next place, oblige it to control itself." It was, of course, the expectations of the founding fathers that this end was, to a degree at least, being accomplished by creating a written constitution as the fundamental law, and by both granting and limiting power through it. Thus Article I lists the powers of Congress ("all legislative powers herein granted. . ."); Article II invests executive power in a President ("the executive power shall be vested in a President. . ."); and Article III confers judicial power to the Courts ("The judicial power of the United States shall be vested in one Supreme Court, and in such inferior Courts as The Congress may from time to time ordain and establish.") Though this separation was itself to act as a limitation on the exercise of governmental power, Article I, section 9, spelled out other specific limitations which were further enlarged by the immediate adoption of the so-called Bill of Rights (Amendments 1–8). And since the States were also agencies with governmental power, Article VI was inserted to give supremacy to the National Government in any conflict with the States while Article I, section 10, further restricted the power of the States in specific instances.

Despite all this, however, the Constitution itself provides no definition either of the powers granted or of the limitations imposed. Nor, for that matter, does it show how the supremacy of the Constitution is to be maintained, or how the governmental machinery set up by Articles I through III is to be made operative so that the true intent of the framers (separation of powers, federalism, limited government, etc.) can be effectuated. If these gaps do exist, and if the

Constitution itself does not provide the organ of government which is to have the definitive role in filling them, how can it be done, and more important still, how is it done? "A dependence on the people," said Madison, "is, no doubt, the primary control on the government, but experience has taught mankind the necessity of auxiliary precautions." Whatever may have been the "experience" that Madison had in mind, or whatever may have been his idea of "auxiliary precautions" the fact remains that the Courts, particularly the Supreme Court, have stepped in, and through the exercise of a power called "Judicial Review," undertaken to protect the Constitution against all enemies, domestic as well as foreign. In doing so, the Supreme Court claimed this power as a matter of right – something inherent in the very nature of the judicial process. The Court might have referred to No. 78 of *The Federalist* wherein Alexander Hamilton specifically claimed it to be the duty of the Court "to declare all acts contrary to the manifest tenor of the Constitution void" but for obvious reasons they preferred this broader ground.

Judicial Review has been defined as the power and duty in a Court (all Courts, inferior and superior; State and Federal) to pass on the validity of legislation (either State or Federal) in specific cases or controversies actually before it and to declare such legislation void if it violates the Constitution of the United States. In the exercise of this power the Court as an institution, and more particularly the judges of the Court, tell us what the Constitution really is. This undoubtedly is what Charles E. Hughes meant when he said, "The Constitution is what the Judges say it is." Do the judges, in telling us what the Constitution is, merely interpret its written provisions (even assuming that such a thing can be done "merely"), or is there more involved? There are to be sure certain self-imposed limits on the exercise of its power (see *Ashwander v. T.V.A.* 297 U.S. 288, 346 [1936] wherein Mr. Justice Brandeis summed up such limits in his concurring opinion) but, by the same token, there can be no doubt that the Justices are inevitably working from principles and policies that affect the whole life of our country, be they political, economic, or social. Small wonder, then, that "Government by Judiciary" is not only the title of many legal volumes (see, for example, Louis B. Boudin "Government by Judiciary" 2 vols., N. Y., 1932) but enters into every discussion concerning a decision that affects both the feelings and interests of large numbers of people and that is of great moment to the Nation as a whole.

While this in itself has caused many much concern, it is immeasurably aggravated when the Court repudiates a principle or policy of long standing. *Stare decisis* (to abide by or adhere to decided cases) is to them more than a legal maxim – it is a Gibraltar of the law's fixity, uniformity, continuity, and certainty. Mr. Justice Douglas has maintained that it is a "healthy consequence of our system when *stare decisis* must give way before the dynamic component of history" for a judge "cannot . . . let men long dead and unaware of the problems of the age in which he lives do his thinking for him." (See his Cardozo Lecture to the New York City Bar Association, April, 1950.) In the same vein Mr. Justice Brandeis in his dissenting opinion in *Burnet v. Coronado Oil and Gas Co.*, 285 U.S. 393 (1932) declared that "*stare decisis* is not . . . a universal, inexorable command. The Court bows to the lessons of experience and the force of better reasoning, recognizing that the process of trial and error, so fruitful in the physical sciences, is appropriate also in the judicial function." And to demonstrate that "This Court has often overruled its earlier decisions" he appends a long list thus citing chapter and verse. Yet the anguish persists for some because such change upsets the coveted anchorage of their vested interests; for others, as Professor Gerald Gunther of Columbia Law School points out, because "there comes a point where a democratic government won't allow an unelected body to substitute its value judgments for those of an elected body"; and for still others because of passions and prejudices and the cries of the momentary majority. But side by side with these are the convictions of some, as Lord Bryce put it, that the Court is "the living voice of the Constitution" or, as Woodrow Wilson put it, that only through the Court can the Constitution be the "vehicle of the Nation's life."

It is, then, through the Supreme Court decision of May 17, 1954, that these battle lines are drawn. The readings in this volume are designed to show how these lines developed and how they are of continuing force insofar as the problem of segregation is concerned. Part I of the readings gives us some necessary background material. The selection from Professor Lon Fuller of the Harvard Law School sets forth the basic philosophies from which a judge, faced with a human problem, can operate in legal terms. The classic case of *Marbury v. Madison* provides the reasoning through which John Marshall went in asserting the Court's power of judicial review, while the case of *Eakin v. Raub* demonstrates that such a conclusion was not inevitable but is rather a political lecture to certain governmental officials. The selection from Charles Warren's monumental work, *The Supreme Court in United States History*, is a general synopsis of how judicial review has actually worked out in practice and the selections from Cardozo and Cushman establish some of the pros and cons of the doctrine as seen by practicing political scientists.

The selections in Part II build up to the 1954 decision in which the Court announced that segregation in the public schools is a denial of equal protection of the laws. The *Dred Scott* case shows the attitude of the Court to the status of the Negro prior to the Civil War; the *Civil Rights Cases* demonstrate the Court's concept of the Negro and his civil rights when Congress tried by legislative action and in pursuance of the 13th and 14th Amendments to safeguard some of these rights; while in *Plessy v. Ferguson* we see how the "separate but equal" doctrine was accepted by the Court as a basic principle with which to deal with the Negro. The excerpt by Leflar and Davis deals with the many possibilities of legal action the Court might have taken while the segregation cases were pending, showing historical precedents as well as current pitfalls. From the brief submitted by the immediate parties to the segregation cases before the Supreme Court comes the next selection which demonstrates the line of argument used by the opposing parties. This is followed by the two principal cases decided by the Court in May of 1954 – one outlawing segregation in the States, and the other in the District of Columbia, which, being under the jurisdiction of the Federal Congress (see Art. I, sec. 8, cl. 17), must be dealt with under the 5th Amendment rather than the 14th. The next three selections are concerned with varying attitudes toward the decisions themselves, focusing essentially on the legal aspects involved.

Part III is designed, as its title indicates, to show the continuing reaction to the Supreme Court decisions – a reaction which covers many fronts. It would, of course, be a mistake to assume that nowhere in the South has the decision been accepted or that integration is still the exception rather than the rule. A recent survey made by the *New York Times* (September, 1957) showed that in Oklahoma, Missouri, Kentucky, West Virginia, and Maryland, a majority of the bi-racial school districts have been integrated; that in Texas, Arkansas, Tennessee, North Carolina, and Delaware, a minority of the bi-racial school districts have been integrated; while in such states as Virginia, Louisiana, Mississippi, Alabama, Georgia, Florida, and South Carolina, no integration has taken place. Despite this, however, the opposition is loud, vocal, and sometimes forceful, and the selections in this section indicate the various forms it has taken. As might be expected the attacks are on two broad levels – attacks on the Court's decisions and attacks on the Court's right to decide. They run the gamut from an objective appraisal of the devices that might be used to evade or delay desegregation, (Leflar and Davis wrote even before the Supreme Court handed down its decisions), to State Resolutions on Interpositions or Nullification, to a Congressional Resolution of Southern Senators dealing with the rights of States, to a political speech (Senator Erwin, D.-N.C.) against the calibre and personnel of the Supreme Court, to a resolution claiming that the 14th Amendment is itself unconstitutional, to proposed amendments leaving education to the exclusive jurisdiction of the States and setting up the Senate as a Supreme Supreme Court, and culminating finally in the use of Federal Armed forces in a State to compel compliance.

The Supreme Court decision is, for the present at least, "the law of the land." The public impact created is due to the breadth of the language employed as well as to the nature and significance of the decision itself. In his "New Reconstruction in the South" (21 *Commentary*, June, 1956, 501–508), C. Vann Woodward emphasizes that the decision has created "a real Constitutional crisis . . . not a sham parade in ancestral costume." Whether it will endure and lead to lasting results (as compared, obviously, to "The failure of the Old Reconstruction") is still an open question. The Negro "Mr. Dooley," Simple, has said of the decision "Great but late" and ponders now "that colored children can run through brickbats to go to school with white children in the South – what's so wonderful about that?" (See Langston Hughes, *Simple Stakes a Claim,* New York, 1957.) President Eisenhower has commented "You cannot change people's hearts merely by laws. Laws . . . express the conscience of a nation and its determination or will to do something." Many Southerners, however, are ready and willing to "launch a crusade against public enemy No. 1" (see advertisement in *The Arkansas Democrat,* Sept. 21, 1957). Perhaps Pascal had the answer when he said, "Justice without might is helpless; might without justice is tyrannical." But in the final analysis this is for each reader to decide for himself.

CONTENTS

I. BACKGROUND

II. SEGREGATION: THE DECISION

The Clash of Issues

I

"There should be no misunderstanding as to the function of this Court. . . . It is sometimes said that the Court assumes a power to overrule or control the action of the people's representatives. This is a misconception. The Constitution is the supreme law of the land ordained and established by the people. All legislation must conform to the principles it lays down. When an act . . . is appropriately challenged in the courts as not conforming to the constitutional mandate, the judicial branch of the Government has only one duty – to lay the article of the Constitution which is involved beside the statute which is challenged and to decide whether the latter squares with the former. All the Court does, or can do, is to announce its considered judgment upon the question. The only power it has, if such it may be called, is the power of Judgment. This Court neither approves nor condemns any legislative policy. Its delicate and difficult office is to ascertain and declare whether the legislation is in accordance with, or in contravention of, the provisions of the Constitution, and having done that, its duty ends. . . ."

– Mr. Justice Roberts in *U.S. v. Butler* – 297 US 1 (1936)

"The power of courts to declare a statute unconstitutional is subject to two guiding principles of decision which ought never to be absent from judicial consciousness. One is that courts are concerned only with the power to enact statutes, not with their wisdom. The other is that while unconstitutional exercise of power by the executive and legislative branches of the government is subject to judicial restraint, the only check upon our own exercise of power is our own sense of self-restraint. For the removal of unwise laws from statute books appeal lies not to the courts but to the ballot and to the processes of democratic government. . . . Courts are not the only agency of government that must be assumed to have capacity to govern. . . ."

– Mr. Justice Stone in his dissenting opinion in
U.S. v. Butler – 297 US 1 (1936)

II

"A constitution, to contain an accurate detail of all the subdivision of which its great powers will admit, and of all the means by which they may be carried into execution, would partake of the prolixity of a legal code, and could scarcely be embraced by the human mind. It would probably never be understood by the public. Its nature, therefore, requires, that only its great outlines should be marked, its important objects designated and the minor ingredients which compose those objects be deduced from the nature of the objects themselves. . . . We must never forget that it is a Constitution we are expounding."

– Chief Justice Marshall in *McCulloch v. Maryland* (1819)

"It is urged that the question involved should now receive fresh consideration, among other reasons, because of the 'economic conditions which have supervened'; but the meaning of the consideration does not change with the ebb and flow of economic events. . . . We frequently are told in more general words that the Constitution must be construed in the light of the present. . . . But to say, if that be intended, that the words of the Constitution mean today what they did not mean when written . . . is to rob that instrument of the essential element which continues it in force as the people have made it until they, and not their official agents, have made it otherwise. . . . The judicial function is that of interpretation; it does not include the power of amendment under the guise of interpretation. To miss the point of difference between the two is to miss all that the phrase 'supreme law of the land' stands for and to convert what was intended as inescapable and enduring mandates into mere moral reflections."

— MR. JUSTICE SUTHERLAND, dissenting in *West Coast Hotel Co. v. Parish,* 300 US 379 (1937)

"In approaching this problem, we cannot turn the clock back to 1868, when the amendment was adopted, or even to 1896 when *Plessy v. Ferguson* was written. . . . Whatever may have been the extent of psychological knowledge at the time of *Plessy v. Ferguson,* this finding (that segregation of white and colored children in public schools has a detrimental effect upon colored children) is amply supported by modern authority. . . ."

— MR. CHIEF JUSTICE WARREN in *Brown et al v. Board of Education of Topeka et al,* 347 US 483 (1954)

III

"We consider the underlying fallacy of the plaintiff's argument to consist in the assumption that the enforced separation of the two races stamps the colored race with a badge of inferiority. . . . The argument also assumes that social prejudices may be overcome by legislation and that equal rights cannot be secured except by an enforced commingling of the two races. We cannot accept this proposition. If the two races are to meet upon terms of social equality, it must be the result of natural affinities, a mutual appreciation of each other's merits and a voluntary consent of individuals. . . . Legislation is powerless to eradicate racial instincts or to abolish distinctions based upon physical differences, and the attempt to do so can only result in accentuating the difficulties of the present situation. . . . If one race be inferior to the other socially, the Constitution of the U.S. cannot put them upon the same plane."

— MR. JUSTICE BROWN in *Plessy v. Ferguson* (1896)

"Our Constitution is color-blind, and neither knows nor tolerates classes among citizens. . . . The arbitrary separation of citizens, on the basis of race . . . in a badge of servitude wholly inconsistent with civil freedom and the equality before the law established by the Constitution. It cannot be justified upon any legal grounds. . . ."

— MR. JUSTICE HARLAN in his dissenting opinion in *Plessy v. Ferguson* (1896)

IV

"The powers of the Federal Government result from a compact to which the States are parties. . . . Each State acceded as a State, and is an integral party, its co-States forming, as to itself, the other party. . . . The government created by this compact was not made the exclusive or final judge of the extent of the powers delegated to itself; since that would make its discretion, and not the Constitution, the measure of its powers. Each State has an equal right to judge for itself, as well of infractions as of the mode and means of redress. . . . In case of a deliberate, palpable, and dangerous exercise of other powers not granted by the said compact, the States, who are parties thereto, have the right and are in duty bound to interpose for arresting the progress of the evil, and for maintaining within their respective limits the authorities, rights, and liberties appertaining to them. . . ."

— The Virginia and Kentucky Resolutions (1798–1799)

"I do not think the United States would come to an end if we lost our power to declare an Act of Congress void. I do think the Union would be imperilled if we could not make that declaration as to the laws of the several states."

— MR. JUSTICE OLIVER WENDELL HOLMES, "Law and the Court" in *Collected Legal Papers,* 295 (1921)

I. BACKGROUND

Lon Fuller: THE CASE OF THE SPELUNCEAN EXPLORERS

In the Supreme Court of Newgarth, 4300

THE defendants, having been indicted for the crime of murder, were convicted and sentenced to be hanged by the Court of General Instances of the County of Stowfield. They bring a petition of error before this court. The facts sufficiently appear in the opinion of the Chief Justice.

TRUEPENNY, C. J. The four defendants are members of the Speluncean Society, an organization of amateurs interested in the exploration of caves. Early in May of 4299 they, in the company of Roger Whetmore, then also a member of the Society, penetrated into the interior of a limestone cavern of the type found in the Central Plateau of this Commonwealth. While they were in a position remote from the entrance to the cave, a landslide occurred. Heavy boulders fell in such a manner as to block completely the only known opening to the cave. When the men discovered their predicament they settled themselves near the obstructed entrance to wait until a rescue party should remove the detritus that prevented them from leaving their underground prison. On the failure of Whetmore and the defendants to return to their homes, the Secretary of the Society was notified by their families. It appears that the explorers had left indications at the headquarters of the Society concerning the location of the cave they proposed to visit. A rescue party was promptly dispatched to the spot.

The task of rescue proved one of overwhelming difficulty. It was necessary to supplement the forces of the original party by repeated increments of men and machines, which had to be conveyed at great expense to the remote and isolated region in which the cave was located. A huge temporary camp of workmen, engineers, geologists, and other experts was established. The work of removing the obstruction was several times frustrated by fresh landslides. In one of these, ten of the workmen engaged in clearing the entrance were killed. The treasury of the Speluncean Society was soon exhausted in the rescue effort, and the sum of eight hundred thousand frelars, raised partly by popular subscription and partly by legislative grant, was expended before the imprisoned men were rescued. Success was finally achieved on the thirty-second day after the men entered the cave.

Since it was known that the explorers had carried with them only scant provisions, and since it was also known that there was no animal or vegetable matter within the cave on which they might subsist, anxiety was early felt that they might meet death by starvation before access to them could be obtained. On the twentieth day of their imprisonment it was learned for the first time that they had taken with them into the cave a portable wireless machine capable of both sending and receiving messages. A similar machine was promptly installed in the rescue camp and oral communication established with the unfortunate men within the mountain. They asked to be informed how long a time would be required to release them. The engineers in charge of the project answered that at least ten days would be required even if no new landslides occurred. The explorers then asked if any physicians were present, and were placed in communication with a committee of medical experts. The imprisoned men described their condition and the rations they had taken with them, and asked for a medical opinion whether they would be likely to live without food for ten days longer. The chairman of the committee of physicians told them that there was little possibility of this. The wireless machine within the cave then remained silent for eight hours. When communication was re-established the men asked to speak again with the physicians. The chairman of the physicians' committee was placed before the apparatus, and Whetmore, speaking on behalf of himself and the defendants asked whether they would be able to survive for ten days longer if they consumed the flesh of one of their number. The physicians' chairman reluctantly answered this question in the affirmative. Whetmore asked whether it would be advisable for them to cast lots to determine which of them should be eaten. None of the physicians present was willing to answer the question. Whetmore then asked if there were among the party a judge or other official of the government who would answer this question. None of those attached to the rescue camp was willing to assume the role of advisor in this matter. He then asked if any minister or priest would answer their question, and none was found who would do so. Thereafter no further messages were received from within the cave, and it was assumed (erroneously, it later appeared) that the electric batteries of the explorers' wireless machine had become exhausted. When the imprisoned men were finally released it was learned that on the twenty-third day after their entrance into the cave Whetmore had been killed and eaten by his companions.

From the testimony of the defendants, which was accepted by the jury, it appears that it was Whetmore who first proposed that they might find the nutriment without which survival was impossible in the flesh of one of their own number. It was also Whetmore who first proposed the use of some method of casting lots, calling the attention of the defendants to a pair of dice he happened to have with him. The defendants were at first reluctant to adopt so desperate a procedure, but after the conversations by wireless related above, they finally agreed on the plan proposed by Whetmore. After much discussion of the mathematical problems involved, agreement was finally reached on a method of determining the issue by the use of the dice.

Before the dice were cast, however, Whetmore declared that he withdrew from the arrangement, as he had decided on reflection to wait for another week before embracing an expedient so frightful and odious. The others charged him with a breach of faith and proceeded to cast the dice. When it came Whetmore's turn, the dice were cast for him by one of the defendants, and he was asked to declare any objections he might have to the fairness of the throw. He stated that he had no such objections. The throw went against him, and he was then put to death and eaten by his companions.

After the rescue of the defendants, and after they had completed a stay in a hospital where they underwent a course of treatment for malnutrition and shock, they were indicted for the murder of Roger Whetmore. At the trial, after the testimony had been concluded, the foreman of the jury (a lawyer by profession) inquired of the court whether the jury might not find a special verdict, leaving it to the court to say whether on the facts as found the defendants were guilty. After some discussion, both the Prosecutor and counsel for the defendants indicated their acceptance of this procedure, and it was adopted by the court. In a lengthy special verdict the jury found the facts as . . . related . . . , and found further that if on these facts the defendants were guilty of the crime charged against them, then they found the defendants guilty. On the basis of this verdict, the trial judge ruled that the defendants were guilty of murdering Roger Whetmore. The judge then sentenced them to be hanged, the law of our Commonwealth permitting him no discretion with respect to the penalty to be imposed. After the release of the jury, its members joined in a communication to the Chief Executive asking that the sentence be commuted to an imprisonment of six months. The trial judge addressed a similar communication to the Chief Executive. As yet no action with respect to these pleas has been taken, as the Chief Executive is apparently awaiting our disposition of this petition of error. . . .

In dealing with this extraordinary case the jury and the trial judge followed a course that was not only fair and wise, but the only course that was open to them under the law. The language of our statute is well known: "Whoever shall willfully take the life of another shall be punished by death." . . . This statute permits of no exception applicable to this case, however our sympathies may incline us to make allowance for the tragic situation in which these men found themselves.

In a case like this the principle of executive clemency seems admirably suited to mitigate the rigors of the law, and I propose to my colleagues that we follow the example of the jury and the trial judge by joining in the communications they have addressed to the Chief Executive. There is every reason to believe that these requests for clemency will be heeded, . . . It is highly improbable that the Chief Executive would deny these requests unless he were himself to hold hearings. . . . Such hearings (which would virtually amount to a retrial of the case) would scarcely be compatible with the function of the Executive as it is usually conceived. I think we may therefore assume that some form of clemency will be extended. . . . If this is done, then justice will be accomplished without impairing either the letter or spirit of our statutes and without offering any encouragement for the disregard of law.

FOSTER, J. I am shocked that the Chief Justice, in an effort to escape the embarrassments of this tragic case, should have adopted, and should have proposed to his colleagues an expedient at once so sordid and so obvious. . . . Something more is on trial in this case than the fate of these unfortunate explorers; that is the law of our Commonwealth. If this Court declares that under our law these men have committed a crime, then our law is itself convicted in the tribunal of common sense, no matter what happens to the individuals involved in this petition of error. For us to assert that the law we uphold and expound compels us to a conclusion we are ashamed of, and from which we can only escape by appealing to a dispensation resting within the personal whim of the Executive, seems to me to amount to an admission that the law of this Commonwealth no longer pretends to incorporate justice.

For myself, I do not believe that our law compels the monstrous conclusion that these men are murderers. I believe, on the contrary, that it declares them to be innocent of any crime. I rest this conclusion. . . . First . . . on a premise that may arouse opposition until it has been examined candidly. I take the view that the enacted or positive law of this Commonwealth, including all of its statutes and precedents, is inapplicable to this case, and that the case is governed instead by what ancient writers in Europe and America called "the law of nature.". . .

Our positive law is predicated on the possibility of men's coexistence in society. When a situation arises in which the coexistence of men becomes impossible, then a condition that underlies all of our precedents and statutes has ceased to exist. . . . Whatever particular objects may be sought by the various branches of our law, it is apparent on reflection that all of them are directed toward facilitating and improving men's coexistence and regulating with fairness and equity the relation of their life in common. . . .

Had the tragic events of this case taken place a mile beyond the territorial limits of our Commonwealth, no one would pretend that our law was applicable to them. . . . Now I contend that a case may be removed morally from the force of a legal order, as well as geographically. If we look to the purpose of law and government, and to the premises underlying our positive law, these men when they made their fateful decision were as remote from our legal order as if they had been a thousand miles beyond our boundaries. Even in a physical sense, their underground prison was separated from our courts and writservers by a solid curtain of rock that could be removed only after the most extraordinary expenditures of time and effort.

I conclude, therefore, that at the time Roger Whetmore's life was ended by these defendants, they were, to use the quaint language of nineteenth-century writers, not in a "state of civil society" but in a "state of nature." This has the consequence that the law applicable to them is not the enacted and established law of this Commonwealth, but the law derived from those principles that were appropriate to their condition. I have no hesitancy in saying that under those principles they were guiltless of any crime.

What these men did was done in pursuance of an agreement accepted by all of them. . . . Since it was apparent that their extraordinary predicament made inapplicable the usual principles that regulate men's relations with one another, it was necessary for them to draw, as it were, a new charter of government appropriate to the situation in which they found themselves.

It has from antiquity been recognized that the most basic principle of law or government is to be found in the notion of contract or agreement. . . . The notion of compact or agreement furnished the only ethical justification on which the powers of government, which include that of taking life, could be rested. The powers of government can only be justified morally on the ground that these are powers that reasonable men would agree upon and accept if they were faced with the necessity of constructing anew some order to make their life in common possible.

* * *

If, therefore, our hangmen have the power to end men's lives, if our sheriffs have the power to put delinquent tenants in the street, if our police have the power to incarcerate the inebriated reveler, these powers find their moral justification in that original compact of our forefathers. If we can find no higher source for our legal order, what higher source should we expect these starving unfortunates to find for the order they adopted for themselves? . . .

The usual conditions of human existence incline us to think of human life as an absolute value, not to be sacrificed under any circumstances. There is much that is fictitious about this conception. . . . We have an illustration of this truth in the very case before us. Ten workmen were killed in the process of removing the rocks from the opening to the cave. . . . If it was proper that these ten lives should be sacrificed to save the lives of five imprisoned explorers, why then are we told it was wrong for these explorers to carry out an arrangement which would save four lives at the cost of one?

Every highway, every tunnel, every building we project involves a risk to human life; . . . statisticians can tell you the average cost in human lives of a thousand miles of a four-lane concrete highway. Yet we deliberately and knowingly incur and pay this cost on the assumption that the values obtained for those who survive outweigh the loss. If these things can be said of a society functioning above ground in a normal and ordinary manner, what shall we say of the supposed absolute value of a human life in the desperate situation in which these defendants . . . found themselves? . . .

I concede for purposes of argument that I am wrong in saying that the situation of these men removed them from the effect of our positive law, and I assume that the Consolidated Statutes have the power to penetrate five hundred feet of rock and to impose themselves upon these starving men huddled in their underground prison.

Now it is, of course, perfectly clear that these men did an act that violates the literal wording of the statute. . . . Every proposition of positive law, whether contained in a statute or a judicial precedent, is to be interpreted reasonably, in the light of its evident purpose. This is a truth so elementary that it is hardly necessary to expatiate on it. Illustrations of its application are numberless and are to be found in every branch of the law. In *Commonwealth* v. *Staymore* the defendant was convicted under a statute making it a crime to leave one's car parked in certain areas for a period longer than two hours. The defendant had attempted to remove his car, but was prevented from doing so because the streets were obstructed by a political demonstration in which he took no part and which he had no reason to anticipate. His conviction was set aside by this Court, although his case fell squarely within the wording of the statute. . . .

The statute before us for interpretation has never been applied literally. Centuries ago it was established that a killing in self-defense is excused. There is nothing in the wording of the statute that suggests this exception. Various attempts have been made to reconcile the legal treatment of self-defense with the words of the statute, but in my opinion these are all merely ingenious sophistries. The truth is that the exception in favor of self-defense cannot be reconciled with the *words* of the statute, but only with its *purpose*.

* * *

One of the principal objects underlying any criminal legislation is that of deterring men from crime. Now it is apparent that if it were declared to be the law that a killing in self-defense is murder such a rule could not operate in a deterrent manner. A man whose life is threatened will repel his aggressor, whatever the law may say. Looking therefore to the broad purposes of criminal legislation, we may safely declare that this statute was not intended to apply to cases of self-defense.

When the rationale of the excuse of self-defense is thus explained, it becomes apparent that precisely the same reasoning is applicable to the case at bar. If in the future any group of men ever find themselves in the tragic predicament of these defendants, we may be sure that their decision whether to live or die will not be controlled by the contents of our criminal code. Accordingly, if we read this statute intelligently it is apparent that it does not apply to this case. . . .

There are those who raise the cry of judicial usurpation whenever a court, after analyzing the purpose of a statute, gives to its words a meaning that is not at once apparent to the casual reader. . . . Let me say emphatically that I accept without reservation the proposition that this Court is bound by the statutes of our Commonwealth and that it exercises its powers in subservience to the duly expressed will of the Chamber of Representatives. The line of reasoning I have applied above raises no question of fidelity to enacted law, though it may possibly raise a question of the distinction between intelligent and unintelligent fidelity. No superior wants a servant who lacks the capacity to read between the lines. The stupidest housemaid knows that when she is told "to peel the soup and skim the potatoes" her mistress does not mean what she says. She also knows that when her master tells her to "drop everything and come running" he has overlooked the possibility that she is at the moment in the act of rescuing the baby from the rain barrel. Surely we have a right to expect the same modicum of intelligence from the judiciary. The correction of obvious legislative errors or oversights is not to supplant the legislative will, but to make that will effective.

I therefore conclude that on any aspect under which this case may be viewed these defendants are innocent of the crime of murdering Roger Whetmore, and that the conviction should be set aside.

TATTING, J. In the discharge of my duties as a justice of this Court, I am usually able to dissociate the emotional and intellectual sides of my reactions, and to decide the case before me entirely on the basis of the latter. In passing on this tragic case I find that my usual resources fail me. On the emotional side I find myself torn between sympathy for these men and a feeling of abhorrence and disgust at the monstrous act they committed. I had hoped that I would be able to put these contradictory emotions to one side as irrelevant, and to decide the case on the basis of a convincing and logical demonstration of the result demanded by our law. Unfortunately, this deliverance has not been vouchsafed me.

* * *

Mr. Justice Foster and I are the appointed judges of a court of the Commonwealth of Newgarth, sworn and empowered to administer the laws of that Commonwealth. By what authority do we resolve ourselves into a Court of Nature? If these men were indeed under the law of nature, whence comes our authority to expound and apply that law? Certainly *we* are not in a state of nature.

* * *

The principles my brother expounds contain other implications that cannot be tolerated. He argues that when the defendants set upon Whetmore and killed him (we know not how, perhaps by pounding him with stones) they were only exercising the rights conferred upon them by their bargain. Suppose, however, that Whetmore had had concealed upon his person a revolver, and that when he saw the defendants about to slaughter him he had shot them to death in order to save his own life. My brother's reasoning applied to these facts would make Whetmore out to be a murderer, since the excuse of self-defense would have to be denied to him. If his assailants were acting rightfully in seeking to bring about his death, then of course he could no more plead the excuse that he was defending his own life than could a condemned prisoner who struck down the executioner lawfully attempting to place the noose about his neck.

* * *

Assuming that we must interpret a statute in the light of its purpose, what are we to do when it has many purposes or when its purposes are disputed? . . .

What are we to do with one of the landmarks of our jurisprudence, which . . . my brother passes over in silence? This is *Commonwealth v. Valjean.* Though the case is somewhat obscurely reported, it appears that the defendant was indicted for the larceny of a loaf of bread, and offered as a defense that he was in a condition approaching starvation. The court refused to accept this defense. If hunger cannot justify the theft of wholesome and natural food, how can it justify the killing and eating of a man? Again, if we look at the thing in terms of deterrence, is it likely that a man will starve to death to avoid a jail sentence for the theft of a loaf of bread? My brother's demonstrations would compel us to overrule *Commonwealth v. Valjean,* and many other precedents that have been built on that case.

Again, I have difficulty in saying that no deterrent effect whatever could be attributed to a decision that these men were guilty of murder. The stigma of the word "murderer" is such that it is quite likely, I believe, that if these men had known that their act was deemed by the law to be murder they would have waited for a few days at least before carrying out their plan. During that time some unexpected relief might have come. . . .

There is still a further difficulty in my brother Foster's proposal to read an exception into the statute to favor this case. . . . Here the men cast lots and the victim was himself originally a party to the agreement. What would we have to decide if Whetmore had refused from the beginning to participate in the plan? Would a majority be permitted to overrule him? Or, suppose that no plan were adopted at all and the others simply conspired to bring about Whetmore's death, justifying their act by saying that he was in the weakest condition. Or again, . . . if the others were atheists and insisted that Whetmore should die because he was the only one who believed in an afterlife. . . .

Should not the soundness of a principle be tested by the conclusions it entails? . . .

I have given this case the best thought of which I am capable. I have scarcely slept since it was argued before us. When I feel myself inclined to accept the view of my brother Foster, I am repelled by a feeling that his arguments are intellectually unsound and approach mere rationalization. On the other hand, when I incline toward upholding the conviction, I am struck by the absurdity of directing that these men be put to death when their lives have been saved at the cost of the lives of ten heroic workmen. It is to me a matter of regret that the Prosecutor saw fit to ask for an indictment for murder. If we had a provision in our statutes making it a crime to eat human flesh, that would have been a more appropriate charge. If no other charge suited to the facts of this case could be brought against the defendants, it would have been wiser, I think, not to have indicted them at all. Unfortunately, however, the men have been indicted and tried, and we have therefore been drawn into this unfortunate affair.

Since I have been wholly unable to resolve the doubts that beset me about the law of this case, I am with regret announcing a step that is, I believe, unprecedented in the history of this tribunal. I declare my withdrawal from the decision of this case.

KEEN, J. I should like to begin by setting to one side two questions which are not before this Court.

The first of these is whether executive clemency should be extended to these defendants if the conviction is affirmed. Under our system of government, that is a question for the Chief Executive, not for us. I therefore disapprove of that passage in the opinion of the Chief Justice in which he in effect gives instructions to the Chief Executive as to what he should do in this case and suggests that some impropriety will attach if these instructions are not heeded. This is a confusion of governmental functions – a confusion of which the judiciary should be the last to be guilty. . . . In the discharge of my duties as judge, it is neither my function to address directions to the Chief Executive, nor to take into account what he may or may not do, in reaching my own decision, which must be controlled entirely by the law of this Commonwealth.

The second question that I wish to put to one side is that of deciding whether what these men did was "right" or "wrong," "wicked" or "good." That is also a question that is irrelevant to the discharge of my office as a judge sworn to apply, not my conceptions of morality, but the law of the land. . . .

The sole question before us for decision is whether these defendants did, . . . willfully take the life of Roger Whetmore. The exact language of the statute is as follows: "Whoever shall willfully take the life of another shall be punished by death." Now I should suppose that any candid observer, content to extract from these words their natural meaning, would concede at once that these defendants did "willfully take the life" of Roger Whetmore.

Whence arise all the difficulties of the case, then, and the necessity for so many pages of discussion about what ought to be so obvious? The difficulties, in whatever tortured form they may present themselves, all trace back to a single source, and that is a failure to distinguish the legal from the moral aspects of this case. To put it bluntly, my brothers do not like the fact that the written law requires the conviction of these defendants. Neither do I, but unlike my brothers I respect the obligations of an office that requires me to put my personal predilections out of my mind when I come to interpret and apply the law of this Commonwealth.

* * *

There was a time in this Commonwealth when judges did in fact legislate very freely, and all of us know that during that period some of our statutes were rather thoroughly made over by the judiciary. . . . We all know the tragic issue of that uncertainty in the brief civil war that arose out of the conflict between the judiciary, on the one hand, and the executive and the legislature, on the other. There is no need to recount here the factors that contributed to that unseemly struggle for power. . . . It is enough to observe that those days are behind us, and that in place of the uncertainty that then reigned we now have a clear-cut principle, which is the supremacy of the legislative branch of our government. From that principle flows the obligation of the judiciary to enforce faithfully the written law, and to interpret that law in accordance with its plain meaning without reference to our personal desires or our individual conceptions of justice. . . .

We are all familiar with the process by which the judicial reform of disfavored legislative enactment is accomplished. . . .

The process of judicial reform requires three steps. The first of these is to divine some single "purpose" which the statute serves. This is done although not one statute in a hundred has any such single purpose, and although the objectives of nearly every statute are differently interpreted by the different classes of its sponsors. The second step is to discover that a mythical being called "the legislator," in the pursuit of this imagined "purpose" overlooked something or left some gap or imperfection in his work. Then comes the final and most refreshing part of the task, which is, to fill in the blank thus created. *Quod erat faciendum.* . . .

One could not wish for a better case to illustrate the specious nature of this gap-filling process than the one before us. My brother thinks he knows exactly what was sought when men made murder a crime, and that was something he calls "deterrence." . . . I doubt very much whether our statute making murder a crime really has a "purpose" in any ordinary sense of the term. Primarily, such a statute reflects a deeply-felt human conviction that murder is wrong and that something should be done to the man who commits it. If we were forced to be more articulate about the matter, we would probably take refuge in the more sophisticated theories of the criminologists, which, of course, were certainly not in the minds of those who drafted our statute. We might also observe that men will do their own work more effectively and live happier lives if they are protected against the threat of violent assault. . . .

If we do not know the purpose, . . . how can we possibly say there is a "gap" in it? How can we know that its draftsmen thought about the question of killing men in order to eat them? My brother Tatting has revealed an understandable, though perhaps slightly exaggerated revulsion to cannibalism. . . . Anthropologists say that the dread felt for a forbidden act may be increased by the fact that the conditions of a tribe's life create special temptations toward it, as incest is most severely condemned among those whose village relations make it most likely to occur. . . .

Now I know that the line of reasoning I have developed in this opinion will not be acceptable to those who look only to the immediate effects of a decision and ignore the long-run implications of an assumption by the judiciary of a power of dispensation. A hard decision is never a popular decision. Judges have been celebrated in literature for their sly prowess in devising some quibble by which a litigant could be deprived of his rights where the public thought it was wrong for him to assert those rights. But

I believe that judicial dispensation does more harm in the long run than hard decisions. Hard cases may even have a certain moral value by bringing home to the people their own responsibilities toward the law that is ultimately their creation, and by reminding them that there is no principle of personal grace that can relieve the mistakes of their representatives.

Indeed, I will go farther and say that not only are the principles I have been expounding those which are soundest for our present conditions, but that we would have inherited a better legal system from our forefathers if those principles had been observed from the beginning. For example, with respect to the excuse of self-defense, if our courts had stood steadfast on the language of the statute the result would undoubtedly have been a legislative revision of it. Such a revision would have drawn on the assistance of natural philosophers and psychologists, and the resulting regulation of the matter would have had an understandable and rational basis, instead of the hodgepodge of verbalisms and metaphysical distinctions that have emerged from the judicial and professorial treatment.

* * *

I conclude that the conviction should be affirmed.

Handy, J. I have listened with amazement to the tortured ratiocinations to which this simple case has given rise. I never cease to wonder at my colleagues' ability to throw an obscuring curtain of legalisms about every issue presented to them for decision. We have heard this afternoon learned disquisitions on the distinction between positive law and the law of nature, the language of the statute and the purpose of the statute, judicial functions and executive functions, judicial legislation and legislative legislation. . . .

What have all these things to do with the case? The problem before us is what we, as officers of the government, ought to do with these defendants. That is a question of practical wisdom, to be exercised in a context, not of abstract theory, but of human realities. When the case is approached in this light, it becomes, I think, one of the easiest to decide that has ever been argued before this Court.

* * *

I have never been able to make my brothers see that government is a human affair, and that men are ruled, not by words on paper or by abstract theories, but by other men. They are ruled well when their rulers understand the feelings and conceptions of the masses. They are ruled badly when that understanding is lacking.

Of all branches of the government, the judiciary is the most likely to lose its contact with the common man. The reasons for this are, of course, fairly obvious. Where the masses react to a situation in terms of a few salient features, we pick into little pieces every situation presented to us. Lawyers are hired by both sides to analyze and dissect. Judges and attorneys vie with one another to see who can discover the greatest number of difficulties and distinctions in a single set of facts. Each side tries to find cases, real or imagined, that will embarrass the demonstrations of the other side. To escape this embarrassment, still further distinctions are invented and imported into the situation. When a set of facts has been subjected to this kind of treatment for a sufficient time, all the life and juice have gone out of it and we have left a handful of dust.

* * *

I believe that all government officials,

including judges, will do their jobs best if they treat forms and abstract concepts as instruments. We should take as our model, I think, the good administrator, who accommodates procedures and principles to the case at hand, selecting from among the available forms those most suited to reach the proper result.

The most obvious advantage of this method of government is that it permits us to go about our daily tasks with efficiency and common sense. My adherence to this philosophy has, however, deeper roots. I believe that it is only with the insight this philosophy gives that we can preserve the flexibility essential if we are to keep our actions in reasonable accord with the sentiments of those subject to our rule. More governments have been wrecked, and more human misery caused, by the lack of this accord between ruler and ruled than by any other factor that can be discerned in history. Once drive a sufficient wedge between the mass of people and those who direct their legal, political, and economic life, and our society is ruined. Then neither Foster's law of nature nor Keen's fidelity to written law will avail us anything.

* * *

This case has aroused an enormous public interest, both here and abroad. Almost every newspaper and magazine has carried articles about it; columnists have shared with their readers confidential information as to the next governmental move; hundreds of letters-to-the-editor have been printed. One of the great newspaper chains made a poll of public opinion on the question, "What do you think the Supreme Court should do with the Speluncean explorers?" About ninety per cent expressed a belief that the defendants should be pardoned or let off with a kind of token punishment. It is perfectly clear, then, how the public feels about the case. We could have known this without the poll, of course, on the basis of common sense, or even by observing that on this Court there are apparently four-and-a-half men, or ninety per cent, who share the common opinion.

This makes it obvious, not only what we should do, but what we must do if we are to preserve between ourselves and public opinion a reasonable and decent accord. Declaring these men innocent need not involve us in any undignified quibble or trick. No principle of statutory construction is required that is not consistent with the past practices of this Court. Certainly no layman would think that in letting these men off we had stretched the statute any more than our ancestors did when they created the excuse of self-defense. . . .

Now I know that my brothers will be horrified by my suggestion that this Court should take account of public opinion. They will tell you that public opinion is emotional and capricious, that it is based on half-truths and listens to witnesses who are not subject to cross-examination. They will tell you that the law surrounds the trial of a case like this with elaborate safeguards, designed to insure that the truth will be known and that every rational consideration bearing on the issues of the case has been taken into account. They will warn you that all of these safeguards go for naught if a mass opinion formed outside this framework is allowed to have any influence on our decision.

But let us look candidly at some of the realities of the administration of our criminal law. When a man is accused of crime, there are, speaking generally, four ways in which he may escape punishment. One of these is a determination by a judge that under the applicable law he has committed no crime. This is, of course, a determination that takes place in a rather formal and abstract atmosphere. But look at the other three ways in which he may escape punishment. These are: (1) a decision by the Prosecutor not to ask for an indictment; (2) an acquittal by the jury; (3) a pardon or commutation of sentence by the Executive. Can anyone pretend that these decisions are held within a rigid and formal framework of rules that prevents factual error, excludes emotional and personal factors, and guarantees that all the forms of the law will be observed?

* * *

I come now to the most crucial fact in this case, a fact known to all of us on this Court, though one that my brothers have seen fit to keep under the cover of their judicial robes. This is the frightening likelihood that if the issue is left to him, the Chief Executive will refuse to pardon these men or commute their sentence. As we all know, our Chief Executive is a man now well advanced in years, of very stiff notions. Public clamor usually operates on him with the reverse of the effect intended. . . .

I must confess that as I grow older I become more and more perplexed at men's refusal to apply their common sense to problems of law and government. . . . I encountered issues like those involved here in the very first case I tried as Judge. . . .

A religious sect had unfrocked a minister who, they said, had gone over to the views and practices of a rival sect. The minister circulated a handbill making charges against the authorities who had expelled him. Certain lay members of the church announced a public meeting at which they proposed to explain the position of the church. The minister attended this meeting. Some said he slipped in unobserved in a disguise; his own testimony was that he had walked in openly as a member of the public. At any rate, when the speeches began he interrupted with certain questions about the affairs of the church and made some statements in defense of his own views. He was set upon by members of the audience and given a pretty thorough pommeling, receiving among other injuries a broken jaw. He brought a suit for damages against the association that sponsored the meeting and against ten named individuals who he alleged were his assailants.

When we came to the trial, the case at first seemed very complicated to me. The attorneys raised a host of legal issues. There were nice questions on the admissibility of evidence, and, in connection with the suit against the association, some difficult problems turning on the question whether the minister was a trespasser or a licensee. As a novice on the bench I was eager to apply my law school learning and I began studying these questions closely, reading all the authorities and preparing well-documented rulings. As I studied the case I became more and more involved in its legal intricacies. . . . Suddenly, however, it dawned on me that all these perplexing issues really had nothing to do with the case, and I began examining it in the light of common sense. The case at once gained a new perspective, and I saw that the only thing for me to do was to direct a verdict for the defendants for lack of evidence.

I was led to this conclusion by the following considerations. The melee in which the plaintiff was injured had been a very confused affair, with some people trying to get to the center of the disturbance, while others were trying to get away from it; some striking at the plaintiff, while others were apparently trying to protect him. It would have taken weeks to find out the truth of the matter. I decided that nobody's broken jaw was worth that much to the Commonwealth. (The minister's injuries, incidentally, had meanwhile healed without disfigurement and without any impairment of normal faculties.) Furthermore, I felt very strongly that the plaintiff had to a large extent brought the thing on himself. He knew how inflamed passions were about the affair, and could easily have found another forum for the expression of his views. My decision was widely approved by the press and public opinion, neither of which could tolerate the views and practices that the expelled minister was attempting to defend.

Now, thirty years later, thanks to an ambitious Prosecutor and a legalistic jury foreman, I am faced with a case that raises issues which are at bottom much like those involved in that case. The world does not seem to change much, except that this time it is not a question of a judgment for five or six hundred frelars, but of the life or death of four men who have already suffered more torment and humiliation than most of us would endure in a thousand years. I conclude that the defendants are innocent of the crime charged, and that the conviction and sentence should be set aside.

* * *

The Supreme Court being evenly divided, the conviction and sentence by the Court of General Instances is *affirmed*. It is ordered that the execution of the sentence shall occur at 6 A.M., Friday, April 2, 4300, at which time the Public Executioner is directed to proceed with all convenient dispatch to hang each of the defendants by the neck until he is dead.

Charles Warren: THE SUPREME COURT IN UNITED STATES HISTORY

THE history of the United States has been written not merely in the halls of Congress, in the Executive offices and on the battlefields, but to a great extent in the chambers of the Supreme Court of the United States. "In the largest proportion of causes submitted to its judgment, every decision becomes a page of history." "In not one serious study of American political life," said Theodore Roosevelt at a dinner of the Bar in honor of Judge Harlan in 1902, "will it be possible to omit the immense part played by the Supreme Court in the creation, not merely the modification, of the great policies, through and by means of which the country has moved on to her present position. . . . The Judges of the Supreme Court of the land must be not only great jurists, they must be great constructive statesmen, and the truth of what I say is illustrated by every study of American statesmanship." The vitally important part, however, which that Court has played in the history of the country in preserving the Union, in maintaining

From *The Supreme Court in United States History* by Charles Warren, Volume I, pages 1–30. By permission of Little, Brown and Company.

National supremacy within the limits of the Constitution, in upholding the doctrines of international law and the sanctity of treaties, and in affecting the trend of the economic, social and political development of the United States, cannot be understood by a mere study of its decisions, as reported in the law books. The Court is not an organism dissociated from the conditions and history of the times in which it exists. It does not formulate and deliver its opinions in a legal vacuum. Its Judges are not abstract and impersonal oracles, but are men whose views are necessarily, though by no conscious intent, affected by inheritance, education and environment and by the impact of history past and present; and as Judge Holmes has said: "The felt necessities of the time, the prevalent moral and political theories, intuitions of public policy, avowed or unconscious, even the prejudices which Judges share with their fellowmen, have had a good deal more to do than the syllogism in determining the rules by which men should be governed."

Appointments to the Court, moreover, have not been made from a cloister of juridical pedants, but from the mass of lawyers and Judges taking active parts in the life of the country. Presidents, in selecting Judges, have been necessarily affected by geographical and political considerations, since it has been desirable that the Court should be representative (so far as practicable) of the different sections of the country and of the leading political parties. The Senate, in rejecting for partisan reasons nominees of eminent legal ability, has more than once influenced the course of history. The character and capacity of counsel taking part in cases have been elements which require consideration, since the arguments of great jurists and great statesmen command an attention and afford an assistance to the Court which may powerfully affect the trend of the law. The reaction of the people to judicially declared law has been an especially important factor in the development of the country; for while the Judges' decision makes law, it is often the people's view of the decision which makes history. Hence, the effect produced upon contemporary public opinion has frequently been of more consequence than the actual decision itself; and in estimating this effect, regard must be paid to the fact that, while the law comes to lawyers through the official reports of judicial decisions, it reaches the people of the country filtered through the medium of the news-columns and editorials of partisan newspapers and often exaggerated, distorted and colored by political comment. Finally, it is to be noted that Congress, in its legislation enacted as a result of judicial decisions, has always played a significant part in relation to the Court. For all these reasons, the true history of the Court must be written not merely from its reported decisions but from the contemporary newspapers, letters, biographies and Congressional debates which reveal its relations to the people, to the States and to Congress, and the reactions of those bodies to its decisions. Recourse to such evidence of contemporary opinion and criticism of the Court is especially necessary for an understanding of the degree to which opposition to the Court and popular counter-movements have affected the history of the country at different periods. Of the great political revolution of 1800 which destroyed the Federalist Party, the public attitude towards the National Judiciary was no small cause. In bringing about the rise of Jacksonian Democracy, the antagonism caused in many States by

John Marshall's decisions was a potent factor. The attitude of the Court on questions arising out of the slavery issue was closely connected with the outbreak of the Civil War. The violent Republican onslaught on the Court for its courageous and notable opinions at the end of the War reacted on the whole unfortunate course of Reconstruction. Nothing in the Court's history is more striking than the fact that, while its significant and necessary place in the Federal form of Government has always been recognized by thoughtful and patriotic men, nevertheless, no branch of the Government and no institution under the Constitution has sustained more continuous attack or reached its present position after more vigorous opposition. It was, however, inevitable from the outset that the Court's powers, its jurisdiction and its decisions should be the subject of constant challenge by one political party or the other; for a tribunal whose chief duty was that of determining between conflicting jurisdictions in a Federal form of Government could not hope to escape criticism, invective, opposition and even resistance. One interesting feature of the first century of its existence should be noted — that the chief conflicts arose over the Court's decisions restricting the limits of State authority and not over those restricting the limits of Congressional power. Discontent with its decisions on the latter subject arose, *not* because the Court held an Act of Congress unconstitutional, but rather because it refused to do so; the Anti-Federalists and the early Republicans assailed the Court because it failed to hold the Sedition Law, the Bank of the United States charter and the Judiciary Act unconstitutional; the Democrats later attacked the Court for enouncing doctrines which would sustain the constitutionality of an Internal Improvement bill, a voluntary Bankruptcy bill, a Protective Tariff bill and similar measures obnoxious to them; the Federalists equally attacked the Court for refusing to hold unconstitutional the Embargo Act, and the later Republicans assailed it for sustaining the Fugitive Slave Act. It was in respect to its exercise of a restraining power over the States that the Court met with its chief opposition. That the Federal Judiciary would of necessity be the focus of attack in all important controversies between the States and the Nation was fully recognized by the framers of the Constitution, but it was the essential pivot of their whole plan. The success of the new Government depended on the existence of a supreme tribunal, free from local political bias or prejudice, vested with power to give an interpretation to Federal laws and treaties which should be uniform throughout the land, to confine the Federal authority to its legitimate field of operation, and to control State aggression on the Federal domain. . . .

The supremacy of the nation in its constitutional field of operation being thus established, [by Article 6 of the Constitution] the next step requisite to the fulfillment of the purposes of the framers of the Constitution was the establishment of a tribunal which should have the power of enforcing throughout the Nation and in the States the supremacy of the Constitution and of the laws so asserted — an organ of Government, which should be, as Bryce has termed it, "the living voice of the Constitution." By the adoption of Sections 1 and 2 of Article III, the framers completed their work in providing that: "The judicial Power of the United States shall be vested in one Supreme Court, and in such inferior Courts as the Congress may from time to time ordain and establish";

and by enumerating the cases to which the judicial power should extend, and the scope of the original and of the appellate jurisdiction of the Supreme Court. The structure of the National Judiciary being thus outlined, the Convention left to the First Congress the important tasks of settling the composition of the Supreme Court, of erecting inferior Courts, of framing modes of procedure, and – most important of all – of establishing the extent of the Supreme Court's appellate jurisdiction, both with reference to State and inferior Federal Courts. The task thus imposed upon the Congress was of a most delicate nature; for during the long contest over the adoption of the Constitution, after it left the hands of its framers, the Article relating to the Judicial branch of the new Government had been the subject of more severe criticism and of greater apprehensions than any other portion of the instrument. Elbridge Gerry had complained that "there are no well-defined limits of the Judiciary powers; they seem to be left as a boundless ocean that has broken over the chart of the Supreme Lawgiver." Edmund Randolph had objected to the lack of limitation or definition of the judicial power. George Mason had said that "the Judiciary of the United States is so constructed and extended as to absorb and destroy the Judiciaries of the several States." Richard Henry Lee had inveighed at length against the powers of the Federal Judiciary. Luther Martin and Patrick Henry had expressed grave fears of the system. On the other hand, the provisions of the Constitution respecting the judicial system had been eloquently supported by Edmund Pendleton, John Marshall, John Jay, James Wilson, James Iredell, James Madison and by Alexander Hamilton, both in speeches at the State Conventions and in pamphlets written in defense of the proposed new Government. . . .

The Judiciary Act was finally enacted on September 24, 1789. It provided for a Supreme Court to consist of a Chief Justice and five Associate Judges; for thirteen District Courts and for three Circuit Courts each to be composed of two Supreme Court Judges sitting with a District Court Judge; it fixed the jurisdiction of the inferior Federal Courts; and it provided for appellate jurisdiction from the State Courts in certain cases presenting Federal questions. With few essential changes, this great piece of legislation has remained the law of the country to the present day. . . .

Later attacks upon the Federal judicial system have been largely attributable to the fact that neither of the two great powers which the Supreme Court has exercised in interpreting and maintaining the supremacy of the Constitution were granted in express terms in the instrument itself. For the power to pass upon the constitutional validity of State legislation was conferred by Congress by this Twenty-Fifth Section of the Judiciary Act, in pursuance of the general power of Congress to pass all acts "necessary and proper for carrying into execution . . . all other powers vested by this Constitution in the Government of the United States," and in order to make effective the provision of Article Six, to the end that the Constitution and the Laws of the United States should be the supreme law of the land. And the Court's power to pass on the constitutional validity of Federal legislation was established by decisions of the Court itself as an inherent and necessary judicial function in ascertaining and interpreting what the finally binding law was. Yet as Madison said in 1832, a supremacy of the Constitution and laws of the Union "without a supremacy in the exposition and execution of them would be as much a mockery as a scabbard put into the hands of a soldier without a sword in it. I have never been able to see that, without such a view of the subject, the Constitution itself could be the supreme law of the land; or that the uniformity of the Federal authority throughout the parties to it could be preserved; or that, without this uniformity, anarchy and disunion could be prevented." The possession of these powers by the Court, moreover, is vital to the preservation not merely of our form of Government, but of the rights and liberties of the individual citizen. "Its exercise," said Judge Field at the Centennial Celebration of the Court, "is necessary to keep the administration of the Government, both of the United States and of the States in all their branches, within the limits assigned to them by the Constitution of the United States and thus secure justice to the people against the unrestrained legislative will of either – the reign of law against the sway of arbitrary power." In any community, the fullness and sufficiency of the securities which surround the individual in the use and enjoyment of his property and his liberty constitute one of the most certain tests of the character and value of the government; and the chief safeguard of the individual's right is to be found in the existence of a Judiciary vested with authority to maintain the supremacy of law above the possession and exercise of governmental power. If the result of an infringement of a written Constitution by the Legislature is to be avoided, "there must be a tribunal to which an immediate appeal for redress can be made by any person who is damnified by the action of the Legislature; and the tribunal which affords redress in such case necessarily exercises judicial power, because it declares what is, and what is not, law, and applies what it declares to be law to the facts submitted to its investigation."

Of the two powers vested in the Court for the enforcement of the supremacy of the Constitution, it may be admitted that its power to pass upon the constitutionality of Congressional legislation was, from the standpoint of the existence of the Nation, of lesser necessity. From 1789 to 1924, forty-nine Acts of Congress were held void; but while the mere existence of the Court's power undoubtedly acted as a legislative deterrent, nevertheless, had the Court not possessed or exercised it, the United States might still have functioned as a Nation. But it must also be noted that, without such power vested in the Court, and with no check on Congress, the Nation could never have remained a Federal Republic. Its government would have become a consolidated and centralized autocracy. Congress would have attained supreme, final and unlimited power over the Executive and the Judiciary branches, and the States and the individual citizens would have possessed only such powers and rights as Congress chose to leave or grant to them. The hard-fought-for Bill of Rights and the reserved powers of the States guaranteed by the Constitution would have become unenforceable. The lives, liberties and properties of the minority would have been subject to the unlimited control of the prejudice, whim or passion of the majority as represented in Congress at any given moment. Though such a government might possibly have operated in this country, it would not have been the form of government which the framers of the Constitution intended, but a government with unlimited powers over the States. Nevertheless, as Judge Holmes has said, "the United States would not come to an end if we lost our power to declare an Act of Congress void." On the other hand, it is unquestionably true that the existence of the United States as a nation would have been endangered, had the Court possessed no power of determining whether State statutes conflicted with the Federal Constitution. "I do think the Union would be imperilled," said Judge Holmes, "if we could not make that declaration as to the laws of the several States. For one in my place sees how often a local policy prevails with those who are not trained to National views. . . . "The power given to the Supreme Court by this (Judiciary) Act," said Chief Justice Taney, "was intended to protect the General Government in the free and uninterrupted exercise of the powers conferred on it by the Constitution, and to prevent any serious impediment from being thrown in its way while acting within the sphere of its legitimate authority." Its great purpose was to avoid conflict of decision between State and Federal authorities, to secure to every litigant whose right depended on Federal law a decision by the Federal Courts, and to prevent the Courts of the several States from impairing the authority of the Federal Government; and had the Court not been vested with this power, it may well be doubted whether the National Union could have been preserved. It was not without reason that John C. Calhoun deemed this Section "the entering wedge," destroying, as he believed, "the relation of co-equals and co-ordinates between the Federal Government and the Governments of the individual States. . . . The effect of this," he said, "is to make the Government of the United States the sole judge, in the last resort, as to the extent of its powers. . . . It is the great enforcing power to compel a State to submit to all acts. . . . Without it, the whole course of the Government would have been different – the conflict between the co-ordinate Governments, in reference to the extent of their respective powers, would have been subject only to the action of the amending power, and thereby the equilibrium of the system been preserved, and the practice of the Government made to conform to its Federal character.". . .

Moreover, it has been through the exercise of this power to pass upon the validity of State statutes, under the Judiciary Act, that the Court has largely controlled and directed the course of the economic and social development of the United States. It is difficult to imagine what the history of the country would have been if there had been no *Dartmouth College Case* on the security of corporate charters; no *McCulloch v. Maryland* on the right of a State to tax a National agency; no *Gibbons v. Ogden* on interstate commerce; no *Brown v. Maryland* or *Passenger Cases* on foreign commerce; no *Craig v. Missouri* on State bills of credit; no *Charles River Bridge Case* on State powers over corporations; no *Slaughter House Cases* on the scope of the Fourteenth Amendment. If it should be answered that, even if this Section did not exist, the question of the validity of a State statute might in some cases have arisen and been determined in suits in the Circuit Courts of the United States, and might have thus reached the Supreme Court from the inferior Federal Courts, this may be admitted; and yet it would have been a slender reed on which to rest the enforcement of the supremacy of the Constitution over conflicting State legislation.

But while it may be truly said that to the existence of the Twenty-Fifth Section of the Judiciary Act may be assigned the chief part of the influence which the Court has had upon the law and the development of the United States, it must be noted as one of the most significant features in the Court's history that the exercise of its powers under this Section has been the chief cause of attack upon the Court itself and upon its decisions.

That the Court should have succeeded in maintaining itself in the confidence and respect of the people in the face of such constant assault is a remarkable tribute to its ability, integrity, independence, and impartiality, and a sign of popular belief in its possession of those qualities. For as an eminent State Judge has well said: "Judicial decisions upon the rights, powers, and attributes of the General and State Government, wherever the Constitution is silent, will often form a topic of much feeling and interest to the people, and of great moment to the Union. So much so, that it has occurred to my mind, as a peculiar and unanswerable reason, arising out of our system of government, why the American Judiciaries both State and Federal, even more than any other judicial tribunals on earth, should be so constituted as to stand independent of temporary excitement and unswayed by pride, popular opinion or party spirit." Fully conscious of this necessity, the Court has time and time again set its face firmly against the appeal of popular passions and prejudices, and the temporary cries of the momentary majority. "The Judiciary of the United States – independent of party, independent of power, and independent of popularity" was a toast given at a dinner in Washington in 1801; these words have expressed the aim, and substantially the achievement, of the Court, in the one hundred and twenty years which have since elapsed. "It is not for Judges to listen to the voice of persuasive eloquence or popular appeal," said Judge Story in the *Dartmouth College Case.* "We have nothing to do but pronounce the law as we find it, and having done this, our justification must be left to the impartial judgment of our country." Loose statements by some modern writers on law and sociology to the effect that the "Bench has always had an avowed partisan bias," are not sustained on examination of its history. Thus, Judges appointed by Jefferson and Madison did not hesitate to join with Marshall in sustaining and developing the strongly Nationalistic interpretation of the Constitution so obnoxious to Jefferson. Judges appointed by Jackson joined with Marshall and Story in supporting the Cherokee Missionaries against Georgia, in flat opposition to Jackson. The whole Bench appointed by Jackson decided against his policy in relation to the Spanish land claims. Judges appointed by Jackson and Van Buren threw down the gauntlet to the former by issuing a mandamus against his favorite Postmaster-General. In every case involving slavery, anti-slavery Judges joined with pro-slavery Judges in rendering the decisions. The constitutionality of the obnoxious Fugitive Slave Law was unanimously upheld by anti-slavery Whig Judges and by pro-slavery Democrats alike. A Southern Democrat joined with a Northern Whig Judge in upholding laws against slave sales. President Lincoln's Legal Tender policy was held unconstitutional by his own appointees. The Reconstruction policies and acts of the Republican Party were held unconstitutional by a Republican Bench. The constitutional views of the Democratic Party as to our insular possessions were opposed by a Democrat Judge who joined with his Republican Associates in making up the majority in the *Insular Cases.* Multiple other illustrations might be cited. In fact, nothing is more striking in the history of the Court than the manner in which the hopes of those who expected a Judge to follow the political views of the President appointing him have been disappointed. While at various periods of extraordinary partisan passion, charges of political motives have been leveled at the Court, it has been generally recognized, when the storms subsided, that the accusations were unwarranted. In fact, it is one of the safeguards of our form of government that the people recognize that the refusal by the Courts to make concessions to expediency or temporary outcry is required for the protection of the rights of the citizen. "Considerate men of every description ought to prize whatever will tend to beget or fortify that temper in the Courts," said Alexander Hamilton, "as no man can be sure that he may not be tomorrow the victim of a spirit of injustice by which he may profit today."...

While ... the Court has won the general confidence of the people, it may fairly be admitted that criticism has not been entirely dissipated, and that temporary resentment over decisions running athwart the opinions of certain classes or sections of the country leads from time to time to demands for changes in the Judiciary system. It has been contended, and with a certain amount of force, that the Court should impose a further voluntary limitation on its power, by announcing that it would decline to regard the unconstitutionality of a statute as "plain," "clear," "palpable" or "unmistakable," in any case in which one or more Judges should consider the statute to be valid; the adoption of such a practice would render impossible most of the "five to four" decisions, which have been so productive of lessened popular respect. It has been suggested that the voluntary elimination or restriction of the now increasing practice of filing dissenting opinions would also tend to strengthen public confidence; on the other hand, such opinions are often of high value in the future development of the law and legislation. More radical suggestions have been made for Constitutional Amendments establishing an elective Court or a Court appointed for a term of years; but such propositions have never yet found any substantial support, since it is manifest that they could only result in making the Judiciary less independent and more politically partisan. Changes have also been suggested in the direction of restricting the appellate jurisdiction of the Court; but such legislation would result in leaving final decision of vastly important National questions in the State or inferior Federal Courts, and would effect a disastrous lack of uniformity in the construction of the Constitution, so that fundamental rights might vary in different parts of the country. As was conclusively said fifty years ago, when the most serious efforts were made thus to weaken the Court; "If the Judges of the Union are silenced, those of the States will be left entirely uncontrolled. Remove the supervisory functions of the National Judiciary, and these laws will become the sport of local partisanship; upheld in one commonwealth, they will be overthrown in another and all compulsive character will be lost. ... To restrict their jurisdiction and weaken their moral power is, therefore, to sacrifice in a most unnecessary manner that department of the Government which more than any other will make National ideas triumphant, not only in the legislation of today but in the permanent convictions of the people." As to the proposition, formerly much advocated, to abolish the Court entirely and to place final power of judicial decision in the United States Senate, no trace of support can now be found.

To the proposal, advanced at various times of intense party passion, that the Court should be increased in number in order to overcome a temporary majority for or against some particular piece of legislation, the good sense of the American people has always given a decided disapproval; even mere partisan politicians see clearly that the employment of such an expedient is a weapon which may be equally used against them by their political opponents and may therefore prove disastrous in the long run; and James Bryce has eloquently set forth the true foundation of the Court's security against such an effort to turn the course of justice: "What prevents such assaults on the fundamental law – assaults which, however immoral in substance, would be perfectly legal in form? Not the mechanism of government, for all its checks have been evaded. Not the conscience of the Legislature and the President, for heated combatants seldom shrink from justifying the means by the end. Nothing but the fear of the people, whose broad good sense and attachment to the great principles of the Constitution may generally be relied on to condemn such a perversion of its forms. Yet if excitement has risen high over the country, a majority of the people may acquiesce; and then it matters little whether what is really a revolution be accomplished by openly violating or by merely distorting the forms of law. To the people we come sooner or later: it is upon their wisdom and self-restraint that the stability of the most cunningly devised scheme of government will in the last resort depend."

No institution of government can be devised which will be satisfactory at all times to all people. But it may truly be said that, in spite of necessary human imperfections, the Court today fulfills its function in our National system better than any instrumentality which has ever been advocated as a substitute. Very apposite are the sentiments expressed by a lawyer in the anxious days of the Republic, just before the *Dred Scott Case*, as follows: "Admit that the Federal Judiciary may in its time have been guilty of errors, that it has occasionally sought to wield more power than was safe, that it is as fallible as every other human institution. Yet it has been and is a vast agency for good; it has averted many a storm which threatened our peace, and has lent its powerful aid in uniting us together in the bonds of law and justice. Its very existence has proved a beacon of safety. And now, when the black cloud is again on the horizon, when the trembling of the earth and the stillness of the air are prophetic to our fears, and we turn to it instinctively for protection, let us ask ourselves, with all its imagined faults, what is there that can replace it? Strip it of its power, and what shall we get in exchange? Discord and confusion, statutes without obedience, Courts without authority, an anarchy of principles, and a chaos of decisions, till all law at last shall be extinguished by an appeal to arms."

From the CONSTITUTION OF THE UNITED STATES

Article I

SECTION 1. All legislative Powers herein granted shall be vested in a Congress of the United States, which shall consist of a Senate and House of Representatives. . . .

Article II

SECTION 1. (1) The executive Power shall be vested in a President of the United States of America. . . .

Article III

SECTION 1. The judicial Power of the United States shall be vested in one supreme Court, and in such inferior Courts as the Congress may from time to time ordain and establish. The Judges, both of the supreme and inferior Courts shall hold their Offices during good Behaviour, and shall, at stated Times, receive for their Services a Compensation, which shall not be diminished during their Continuance in Office.

SECTION 2. (1) The judicial Power shall extend to all Cases, in Law and Equity, arising under this Constitution, the Laws of the United States, and Treaties made, or which shall be made, under their Authority; — to all Cases affecting Ambassadors, other public Ministers and Consuls; — to all Cases of admiralty and maritime Jurisdiction; — to Controversies to which the United States shall be a Party; — to Controversies between two or more States; — *between a State and Citizens of another State;*[*] — between Citizens of different States; — between Citizens of the same State claiming Lands under Grants of different States, and between a State, or the Citizens thereof, and foreign States, Citizens or Subjects.

(2) In all Cases affecting Ambassadors, other public Ministers and Consuls, and those in which a State shall be Party, the supreme Court shall have original Jurisdiction. In all the other Cases before mentioned, the supreme Court shall have appellate Jurisdiction, both as to Law and Fact, with such Exceptions, and under such Regulations as the Congress shall make. . . .

Article VI

(2) This Constitution, and the Laws of the United States which shall be made in Pursuance thereof; and all Treaties made, or which shall be made, under the Authority of the United States, shall be the supreme Law of the Land; and the Judges in every State shall be bound thereby, any Thing in the Constitution or Laws of any State to the Contrary notwithstanding.

(3) The Senators and Representatives before mentioned, and the Members of the several State Legislatures, and all executive and judicial Officers, both of the United States and of the several States shall be bound by Oath or Affirmation, to support this Constitution; . . .

[*] [Restricted by the Eleventh Amendment. ED.]

MARBURY *v.* MADISON

[President Adams nominated, and appointed by and with the advice and consent of the Senate, William Marbury to be justice of the peace for the county of Washington in the District of Columbia. Marbury's commission was signed and sealed in due form, but was not delivered before President Adams' term of office expired. His successor in office, President Jefferson, instructed James Madison, Secretary of State, to withhold Marbury's commission. Marbury sought a writ of *mandamus* against Madison to compel delivery.]

Chief Justice Marshall delivered the opinion of the Court.

* * *

IN the order in which the court viewed this subject, the following questions have been considered and decided.

1st. Has the applicant a right to the commission he demands? [The court finds that he has, and that the right has been violated.]

2dly. If he has a right, and that right has been violated, do the laws of his country afford him a remedy? [The Court finds that they do.]

3dly. If they do afford him a remedy, is it a *mandamus* issuing from this court? [The Court finds the *mandamus* an appropriate remedy.]

This, then, is a plain case for a *mandamus* . . . and it only remains to be inquired,

Whether it can issue from this court.

The act [of Congress] to establish the judicial courts of the United States authorizes the supreme court "to issue writs of *mandamus,* in cases warranted by the principles and usages of law, to any courts appointed, or persons holding office, under the authority of the United States."

The secretary of state, being a person holding an office under the authority of the United States, is precisely within the letter of the description; and if this court is not authorized to issue a writ of *mandamus* to such an officer, it must be because the law is unconstitutional. . . .

The constitution vests the whole judicial power of the United States in one supreme court, and such inferior courts as congress shall, from time to time, ordain and establish. . . .

In the distribution of this power it is declared that "the supreme court shall have original jurisdiction in all cases affecting ambassadors, other public ministers and consuls, and those in which a State shall be a party. In all other cases, the supreme court shall have appellate jurisdiction.". . .

If Congress remains at liberty to give this court appellate jurisdiction, where the constitution has declared their jurisdiction shall be original; and original jurisdiction where the constitution has declared it shall be appellate; the distribution of jurisdiction, made in the constitution, is form without substance. . . .

It cannot be presumed that any clause in the constitution is intended to be without effect; and, therefore, such a construction is inadmissible, unless the words require it. . . .

To enable this court, then, to issue a *mandamus,* it must be shown to be an

1 Cranch 137 [1803]

exercise of appellate jurisdiction, or to be necessary to enable them to exercise appellate jurisdiction. . . .

The authority, therefore, given to the supreme court, by the act establishing the judicial courts of the United States, to issue writs of *mandamus* to public offices, appears not to be warranted by the constitution; and it becomes necessary to inquire whether a jurisdiction so conferred can be exercised.

The question, whether an act repugnant to the constitution can become the law of the land, is a question deeply interesting to the United States. . . .

That the people have an original right to establish, for their future government, such principles as, in their opinion, shall most conduce to their own happiness, is the basis on which the whole American fabric has been erected. . . . The principles, therefore, so established, are deemed fundamental. And as the authority from which they proceed is supreme, and can seldom act, they are designed to be permanent.

This original and supreme will organizes the government, and assigns to different departments their respective powers. It may either stop here, or establish certain limits not to be transcended by those departments.

The government of the United States is of the latter description. The powers of the legislature are defined and limited; and that those limits may not be mistaken, or forgotten, the constitution is written. To what purpose are powers limited, and to what purpose is that limitation committed to writing, if these limits may, at any time, be passed by those intended to be restrained? The distinction between a government with limited and unlimited powers is abolished, if those limits do not confine the persons on whom they are imposed, and if acts prohibited and acts allowed, are of equal obligation. It is a proposition too plain to be contested, that the constitution controls any legislative act repugnant to it; or, that the legislature may alter the constitution by an ordinary act.

Between these alternatives there is no middle ground. The constitution is either a superior paramount law, unchangeable by ordinary means, or it is on a level with ordinary legislative acts, and, like other acts, is alterable when the legislature shall please to alter it.

If the former part of the alternative is true, then a legislative act contrary to the constitution, is not law; if the latter part be true, then written constitutions are absurd attempts, on the part of the people, to limit a power in its own nature illimitable.

Certainly all those who have framed written constitutions contemplate them as forming the fundamental and paramount law of the nation, and, consequently, the theory of every such government must be, that an act of the legislature, repugnant to the constitution, is void.

This theory is essentially attached to a written constitution, and is consequently to be considered, by this court, as one of the fundamental principles of our society. It is not, therefore, to be lost sight of in the further consideration of this subject.

If an act of the legislature, repugnant to the constitution, is void, does it, notwithstanding its invalidity, bind the courts, and oblige them to give it effect? Or, in other words, though it be not law, does it constitute a rule as operative as if it was a law? This would be to overthrow in fact what was established in theory; and would seem, at first view, an absurdity too gross to be insisted on. It shall, however, receive a more attentive consideration.

It is emphatically the province and duty of the judicial department to say what the law is. Those who apply the rule to particular cases, must of necessity expound and interpret the rule. If two laws conflict with each other, the courts must decide on the operation of each.

So if a law be in opposition to the constitution; if both the law and the constitution apply to a particular case, so that the court must either decide that case conformably to the law, disregarding the constitution, or conformably to the constitution, disregarding the law, the court must determine which of these conflicting rules governs the case. This is of the very essence of judicial duty.

If, then, the courts are to regard the constitution, and the constitution is superior to any ordinary act of the legislature, the constitution, and not such ordinary act, must govern the case to which they both apply.

Those, then, who controvert the principle that the constitution is to be considered, in court, as a paramount law, are reduced to the necessity of maintaining that courts must close their eyes on the constitution, and see only the law.

This doctrine would subvert the very foundation of all written constitutions. It would declare that an act which, according to the principles and theory of our government, is entirely void, is yet, in practice, completely obligatory. It would declare that if the legislature shall do what is expressly forbidden, such act, notwithstanding the express prohibition, is in reality effectual. It would be giving to the legislature practical and real omnipotence, with the same breath which professes to restrict their powers within narrow limits. It is prescribing limits, and declaring that those limits may be passed at pleasure.

That it thus reduces to nothing what we have deemed the greatest improvement on political institutions, a written constitution, would of itself be sufficient, in America, where written constitutions have been viewed with so much reverence, for rejecting the construction. But the peculiar expressions of the constitution of the United States furnish additional arguments in favor of its rejection.

The judicial power of the United States is extended to all cases arising under the constitution.

Could it be the intention of those who gave this power, to say that in using it the constitution should not be looked into? That a case arising under the constitution should be decided without examining the instrument under which it arises?

This is too extravagant to be maintained.

In some cases, then, the constitution must be looked into by the judges. And if they can open it at all, what part of it are they forbidden to read or to obey?

There are many other parts of the constitution which serve to illustrate this subject.

It is declared that "no tax or duty shall be laid on articles exported from any State." Suppose a duty on the export of cotton, of tobacco, or of flour; and a suit instituted to recover it. Ought judgment to be rendered in such a case? Ought the judges to close their eyes on the constitution and only see the law?

The constitution declares "that no bill of attainder or *ex post facto* law shall be passed."

If, however, such a bill should be passed, and a person should be prosecuted under it, must the court condemn to death those victims whom the constitution endeavors to preserve?

"No person," says the constitution,

"shall be convicted of treason unless on the testimony of two witnesses to the same overt act, or on confession in open court."

Here the language of the constitution is addressed especially to the courts. It prescribes, directly for them, a rule of evidence not to be departed from. If the legislature should change that rule, and declare one witness, or a confession out of court, sufficient for conviction, must the constitutional principle yield to the legislative act?

From these, and many other selections which might be made, it is apparent that the framers of the constitution contemplated that instrument as a rule for the government of courts, as well as of the legislature.

Why otherwise does it direct the judges to take an oath to support it? This oath certainly applies in an especial manner to their conduct in their official character. . . .

The oath of office, too, imposed by the legislature, is completely demonstrative of the legislative opinion on this subject. It is in these words: "I do solemnly swear that I will administer justice without respect to persons, and do equal right to the poor and to the rich; and that I will faithfully and impartially discharge all the duties incumbent on me as . . . , according to the best of my abilities and understanding, agreeably to the constitution and laws of the United States."

Why does a judge swear to discharge his duties agreeably to the constitution of the United States, if that constitution forms no rule for his government — if it is closed upon him, and cannot be inspected by him?

If such be the real state of things, this is worse than solemn mockery. To prescribe, or to take this oath, becomes equally a crime.

It is also not entirely unworthy of observation, that in declaring what shall be the supreme law of the land, the constitution itself is first mentioned; and not the laws of the United States generally, but those only which shall be made in pursuance of the constitution, have that rank.

Thus, the particular phraseology of the constitution of the United States confirms and strengthens the principle, supposed to be essential to all written constitutions, that a law repugnant to the constitution is void; and that courts, as well as other departments, are bound by that instrument.

EAKIN *v.* RAUB

GIBSON, J. . . . I am aware, that a right [in the judiciary] to declare all unconstitutional acts void . . . is generally held as a professional dogma; but, I apprehend, rather as a matter of faith than of reason. I admit that I once embraced the same doctrine, but without examination, and I shall therefore state the arguments that impelled me to abandon it, with great respect for those by whom it is still maintained. But I may premise, that it is not a little remarkable, that although the right in question has all along been claimed by the judiciary, no judge has ventured to discuss it, except Chief Justice MARSHALL, and if the argument of a jurist so distinguished for the strength of his ratiocinative powers be

12 Sergeant and Rawle (Pennsylvania Supreme Court) 330. (1825)

found inconclusive, it may fairly be set down to the weakness of the position which he attempts to defend. . . .

I begin, then, by observing that in this country, the powers of the judiciary are divisible into those that are POLITICAL and those that are purely CIVIL. Every power by which one organ of the government is enabled to control another, or to exert an influence over its acts, is a political power. . . . [The judiciary's] civil, are its *ordinary* and *appropriate* powers; being part of its essence, and existing independently of any supposed grant in the constitution. But where the government exists by virtue of a *written* constitution, the judiciary does not necessarily derive from that circumstance, any other than its ordinary and appropriate powers. Our judiciary is constructed on the principles of the common law, which enters so essentially into the composition of our social institutions as to be inseparable from them, and to be, in fact, the basis of the whole scheme of our civil and political liberty. In adopting any organ or instrument of the common law, we take it with just such powers and capacities as were incident to it at the common law, except where these are expressly, or by necessary implication, abridged or enlarged in the act of adoption; and, that such act is a written instrument, cannot vary its consequences or construction. . . . Now, what are the powers of the judiciary at the common law? They are those that necessarily arise out of its immediate business; and they are therefore commensurate only with the judicial execution of the municipal law, or, in other words, with the administration of distributive justice, without extending to anything of a political cast whatever. . . . With us, although the legislature be the depository of only so much of the sovereignty as the people have thought fit to impart, it is nevertheless sovereign within the limit of its powers, and may relatively claim the same pre-eminence here that it may claim elsewhere. It will be conceded, then, that the ordinary and essential powers of the judiciary do not extend to the annulling of an act of the legislature. . . .

The constitution and the right of the legislature to pass the act, may be in collision. But is that a legitimate subject for judicial determination? If it be, the judiciary must be a peculiar organ, to revise the proceedings of the legislature, and to correct its mistakes; and in what part of the constitution are we to look for this proud pre-eminence? Viewing the matter in the opposite direction, what would be thought of an act of assembly in which it should be declared that the supreme court had, in a particular case, put a wrong construction on the constitution of the United States, and that the judgment should therefore be reversed? It would doubtless be thought a usurpation of judicial power. But it is by no means clear, that to declare a law void which has been enacted according to the forms prescribed in the constitution is not a usurpation of legislative power. It is an act of sovereignty; and sovereignty and legislative power are said by Sir William Blackstone to be convertible terms. It is the business of the judiciary to interpret the laws, not scan the authority of the lawgiver; and without the latter, it cannot take cognizance of a collision between a law and the Constitution. So that to affirm that the judiciary has a right to judge of the existence of such collision, is to take for granted the very thing to be proved. And, that a very cogent argument may be made in this way, I am not disposed to deny; for no conclusions are so strong as those that are drawn from the petitio principii.

But it has been said to be emphatically the business of the judiciary to ascertain and pronounce what the law is; and that this necessarily involves a consideration of the constitution. It does so: but how far? If the judiciary will inquire into anything besides the form of enactment, where shall it stop? There must be some point of limitation to such an inquiry; for no one will pretend that a judge would be justifiable in calling for the election returns, or scrutinizing the qualifications of those who composed the legislature. . . .

In theory, all the organs of the government are of equal capacity; or, if not equal, each must be supposed to have superior capacity only for those things which peculiarly belong to it; and, as legislation peculiarly involves the consideration of those limitations which are put on the law-making power, and the interpretation of the laws when made, involves only the construction of the laws themselves, it follows that the construction of the constitution in this particular belongs to the legislature, which ought therefore to be taken to have superior capacity to judge of the constitutionality of its own acts. But suppose all to be of equal capacity in every respect, why should one exercise a controlling power over the rest? That the judiciary is of superior rank, has never been pretended, although it has been said to be co-ordinate. It is not easy, however, to comprehend how the power which gives law to all the rest, can be of no more than equal rank with one which receives it, and is answerable to the former for the observance of its statutes. Legislation is essentially an act of sovereign power; but the execution of the laws by instruments that are governed by prescribed rules and exercise no power of volition, is essentially otherwise. . . . It may be said, the power of the legislature, also, is limited by prescribed rules. It is so. But it is, nevertheless, the power of the people, and sovereign as far as it extends. It cannot be said, that the judiciary is co-ordinate merely because it is established by the constitution. If that were sufficient, sheriffs, registers of wills, and recorders of deeds, would be so too. Within the pale of their authority, the acts of these officers will have the power of the people for their support; but no one will pretend they are of equal dignity with the acts of the legislature. Inequality of rank arises not from the manner in which the organ has been constituted, but from its essence and the nature of its functions; and the legislative organ is superior to every other, inasmuch as the power to will and to command, is essentially superior to the power to act and to obey. . . .

Everyone knows how seldom men think exactly alike on ordinary subjects; and a government constructed on the principle of assent by all its parts, would be inadequate to the most simple operations. The notion of a complication of counter checks has been carried to an extent in theory, of which the framers of the constitution never dreamt. When the entire sovereignty was separated into its elementary parts, and distributed to the appropriate branches, all things incident to the exercise of its powers were committed to each branch exclusively. The negative which each part of the legislature may exercise, in regard to the acts of the other, was thought sufficient to prevent material infractions of the restraints which were put on the power of the whole; for, had it been intended to interpose the judiciary as an additional barrier, the matter would surely not have been left in doubt. The judges would not have been left to stand on the insecure and ever shifting ground of public opinion as to constructive powers; they would have been placed on the impregnable ground of an express grant. They would not have been compelled to resort to the debates in the convention, or the opinion that was generally entertained at the time. A constitution, or a statute, is supposed to contain the whole will of the body from which it emanated; and I would just as soon resort to the debates in the legislature for the construction of an act of assembly, as to the debates in the convention for the construction of the constitution.

The power is said to be restricted to cases that are free from doubt or difficulty. But the abstract existence of a power cannot depend on the clearness or obscurity of the case in which it is to be exercised; for that is a consideration that cannot present itself before the question of the existence of the power shall have been determined; and, if its existence be conceded, no considerations of policy arising from the obscurity of the particular case ought to influence the exercise of it. . . .

To say, therefore, that the power is to be exercised but in perfectly clear cases, is to betray a doubt of the propriety of exercising it at all. Were the same caution used in judging of the existence of the power that is inculcated as to the exercise of it, the profession would perhaps arrive at a different conclusion. The grant of a power so extraordinary ought to appear so plain, that he who should run might read. . . .

But the judges are sworn to support the Constitution, and are they not bound by it as the law of the land? In some respects they are. In the very few cases in which the judiciary, and not the legislature, is the immediate organ to execute its provisions, they are bound by it in preference to any act of assembly to the contrary. In such cases, the Constitution is a rule to the courts. What I have in view in this inquiry, is the supposed right of the judiciary to interfere in cases where the constitution is to be carried into effect through the instrumentality of the legislature, and where that organ must necessarily first decide on the constitutionality of its own act. The oath to support the constitution is not peculiar to the judges, but is taken indiscriminately by every officer of the government, and is designed rather as a test of the political principles of the man, than to bind the officer in the discharge of his duty: otherwise it is difficult to determine what operation it is to have in the case of a recorder of deeds, for instance, who, in the execution of his office, has nothing to do with the constitution. But granting it to relate to the official conduct of the judge, as well as every other officer, and not to his political principles, still it must be understood in reference to supporting the constitution, *only as far as that may be involved in his official duty;* and, consequently, if his official duty does not comprehend an inquiry into the authority of the legislature, neither does his oath. It is worthy of remark here, that the foundation of every argument in favor of the right of the judiciary is found at last to be an assumption of the whole ground in dispute. Granting that the object of the oath is to secure a support of the Constitution in the discharge of official duty, its terms may be satisfied by restraining it to official duty in the exercise of the ordinary judicial powers. Thus, the Constitution may furnish a rule of construction, where a particular interpretation of a law would conflict with some constitutional principle; and such interpretation, where it may, is always to be avoided. But the oath was more probably designed to secure the powers of each of the different branches from being usurped by any of the rest: for instance, to prevent the House of Representatives from erecting itself into a court of judicature, or the Supreme Court from attempting to control the legislature; and, in this view, the oath furnishes an argument equally plausible against the right of the judiciary. But if it require a support of the Constitution in anything beside official duty, it is in fact an oath of allegiance to a particular form of government; and, considered as such, it is not easy to see why it should not be taken by the citizens at large, as well as by the officers of the government. It has never been thought that an officer is under greater restraint as to measures which have for their avowed end a total change of the Constitution, than a citizen who has taken no oath at all. The official oath, then, relates only to the official conduct of the officer, and does not prove that he ought to stray from the path of his ordinary business to search for violations of duty in the business of others; nor does it, as supposed, define the powers of the officer.

But do not the judges do a positive act in violation of the constitution, when they give effect to an unconstitutional law? Not if the law has been passed according to the forms established in the constitution. The fallacy of the question is in supposing that the judiciary adopts the acts of the legislature as its own; whereas the enactment of a law and the interpretation of it are not concurrent acts, and as the judiciary is not required to concur in the enactment, neither is it in the breach of the constitution which may be the consequence of the enactment. The fault is imputable to the legislature, and on it the responsibility exclusively rests. . . .

But it has been said, that this construction would deprive the citizen of the advantages which are peculiar to a written constitution, by at once declaring the power of the legislature in practice to be illimitable. . . . But there is no magic or inherent power in parchment and ink, to command respect and protect principles from violation. In the business of government a recurrence to first principles answers the end of an observation at sea with a view to correct the dead reckoning; and for this purpose, a written constitution is an instrument of inestimable value. It is of inestimable value, also, in rendering its first principles familiar to the mass of people; for, after all, there is no effectual guard against legislative usurpation but public opinion, the force of which, in this country, is inconceivably great. . . . Once let public opinion be so corrupt as to sanction every misconstruction of the constitution and abuse of power which the temptation of the moment may dictate, and the party which may happen to be predominant will laugh at the puny efforts of a dependent power to arrest it in its course.

For these reasons, I am of opinion that it rests with the people, in whom full and absolute sovereign power resides, to correct abuses in legislation, by instructing their representatives to repeal the obnoxious act. What is wanting to plenary power in the government is reserved by the people for their own immediate use; and to redress an infringement of their rights in this respect would seem to be an accessory of the power thus reserved. It might, perhaps, have been better to vest the power in the judiciary; as it might be expected that its habits of deliberation, and the aid derived from the arguments of counsel, would more frequently lead to accurate conclusions. On the other hand, the judiciary is not infallible; and an error by it would admit of no remedy but a more distinct expression of the public will, through the extraordinary medium of a convention; whereas, an error by the legislature admits of a remedy by an exertion of the same will, in the ordinary exercise of the right of suffrage, a mode better calculated to attain the end, without popular excitement. It may be said, the people would probably not notice an error of their representatives. But they would as probably do so as notice an error of the judiciary; and, besides, it is a postulate in the theory of our government, and the very basis of the superstructure, that the people are wise, virtuous, and competent to manage their own affairs; and if they are not so, in fact, still every question of this sort must be determined according to the principles of the constitution, as it came from the hands of the framers, and the existence of a defect which was not foreseen would not justify those who administer the government, in applying a corrective in practice, which can be provided only by convention. . . .

But in regard to an act of [a state] assembly,* which is found to be in collision with the constitution, laws, or treaties of the *United States,* I take the duty of the judiciary to be exactly the reverse. By becoming parties to the federal constitution, the states have agreed to several limitations of their individual sovereignty, to enforce which, it was thought to be absolutely necessary to prevent them from giving effect to laws in violation of those limitations, through the instrumentality of their own judges. Accordingly, it is declared in the sixth article and second section of the federal constitution, that "This constitution, and the laws of the *United States* which shall be made in pursuance thereof, and all treaties made, or which shall be made under the authority of the *United States,* shall be the *supreme* law of the land; and the *judges* in every *state* shall be BOUND thereby; anything in the *Constitution* or *laws* of any *state* to the contrary notwithstanding."

This is an express grant of a political power, and it is conclusive to show that no law of inferior obligation, as every state law must necessarily be, can be executed at the expense of the constitution, laws, or treaties of the *United States.* It may be said, these are to furnish a rule only when there is no state provision on the subject. But, in that view, they could with no propriety be called supreme; for supremacy is a relative term, and cannot be predicted of a thing which exists separately and alone: and this law, which is called supreme, would change its character and become subordinate as soon as it should be found in conflict with a state law. But the judges are to be bound by the federal constitution and laws, notwithstanding anything in the constitution or laws of the particular state *to the contrary.* If, then, a state were to declare the laws of the *United States* not to be obligatory on her judges, such an act would unquestionably be void; for it will not be pretended, that any member of the union can dispense with the obligation of the federal constitution: and, if it cannot be done directly, and by a general declaratory law, neither can it indirectly, and by by-laws dispensing with it in particular cases. . . .

* [See Fletcher v. Peck, 6 Cranch 87 (1810). Ed.]

Robert E. Cushman: THE ROLE OF A SUPREME COURT IN A DEMOCRATIC NATION

CAN the Supreme Court be divested of its undemocratic assumption of legislative power? . . . How can we establish a sounder and more democratic balance between the legislative and judicial powers under the American Constitution? I have two answers to this question, . . .

The first of my proposals is a very simple and wholly unspectacular one. It does not upset anything and it would, I believe, increase rather than weaken the Court's prestige. It is the simple proposal that the Court shall of its own volition abandon the job of legislating and confine itself to the task of judging; that in reviewing legislation it shall accord what Mr. Justice Washington over a hundred years ago called "a decent respect due to the legislative body by which any law is passed." This is, of course, exactly what the Supreme Court officially claims that it does, and no one would endorse my suggestion more heartily, in all probability, than those justices who have been among the most ruthless in overriding legislation on the basis of "personal economic predilections."

But what I have in mind is not a matter of words. It is a thing of the spirit, a positive and aggressive determination on the part of the Court to encroach just as little as possible upon legislative discretion, a complete unwillingness to invalidate a statute if any reasonable ground can be discovered upon which it may be sustained. This was the life-long judicial philosophy of Mr. Justice Holmes. Justices Brandeis, Cardozo, and Stone . . . [also upheld] this doctrine of judicial tolerance. It claim[ed] the adherence of Chief Justice Hughes not infrequently and of Mr. Justice Roberts once in a while. This attitude is peculiarly necessary in applying the nebulous test of due process of law to social and economic legislation. Whether such legislation is "arbitrary" or not, is, after all, a matter of opinion and the legislature is entitled to its opinion even if that opinion be mistaken or foolish. "There is nothing that I more deprecate," said Mr. Justice Holmes, "than the use of the Fourteenth Amendment beyond the absolute compulsion of its words to prevent the making of social experiments that an important part of the community desires, in the insulated chambers afforded by the several states, even though the experiments may seem futile or even noxious to me and to those whose judgment I most respect." There is certain irony in the fact that Holmes came to be universally regarded as a great liberal. Every advocate of social and economic reform regarded him as an ally. And so he was – but not always in the sense in which they thought him to be. There is reason to believe that Holmes had little use for a large amount of the social and economic reform which he voted to hold constitutional. In his own social philosophy he was a fairly conservative man. But he believed firmly in two things – first, as he neatly put it, "I am not God"; second, an American legislature possesses what Lowell called in the Bigelow Papers "the right to be a cussed fool," and that right must be respected and protected by the Supreme Court. Holmes's liberalism was the

Robert E. Cushman, Edmund J. James Lecture at the University of Illinois, March 9, 1938. Reprinted with the permission of the University of Illinois Press and Professor Cushman.

liberalism of tolerance, often a disgusted tolerance, a tolerance grounded on respect for the integrity of the legislature's own job no matter how stupidly that job was done. That attitude on the part of the Court is vitally necessary at the present time. Its attainment and the development of a tradition which would make it permanent would do more to restore the Supreme Court to its proper place in the American Constitutional system than any of the drastic proposals which I mentioned and discarded a moment ago.

Is there any hope of securing such an attitude upon the part of the Court towards legislation? I believe there is even if results of this somewhat intangible sort may not be achieved all at once. There are two ways in which progress may be made. One is by the slow process of education. This means education within the legal profession so that lawyers who attain seats on the Bench will have a sound and wise understanding of the nature of the judge's job with respect to legislation. It means education in a broader base so that there may be an increasingly well informed public opinion to insist upon the appointment to the Bench of men who have this attitude. We are beginning to profit from the results of this educational movement which has been going on for twenty years or more. A second way in which progress may be made is by focusing attention and public pressure upon the Presidential appointment of judges of the right kind and upon their confirmation by the Senate. . . . Our existing system of choosing Supreme Court justices does not give us as good results as it should. We get a few distinguished men, a good many able men, and now and again somebody definitely below par. The country is entitled to have on the Bench judicial statesmen. The traditions surrounding Supreme Court appointments must be so shaped as to secure them. It must be made good politics for the President to name such men and for the Senate to confirm them. The making of these vitally important appointments should never be casually inadvertent. It might be wise if the rules of the Senate should forbid the confirmation of major judicial appointments in less than thirty days so that full and open hearings may be had upon the qualifications of the men named by the President. Progress along these lines may be slow and erratic, but I believe that public opinion in this country is coming to see the importance of securing the right kind of Supreme Court justices and that we shall build up the kind of traditions which will insure their appointment.

I have a second proposal to make. This we may fall back on if we fail to persuade the Supreme Court to abdicate voluntarily its legislative and policy-determining functions and to adopt the wise tolerance toward legislative discretion which Mr. Justice Holmes preached and practiced. This proposal is that we adopt clarifying amendments to the Constitution which will sharpen the meaning of its clauses, make clear the scope of its delegations of power, and the impact of its limitations. The Court in construing the commerce clause or the due process clause is engaged in making broad decisions of policy which do not properly belong to a judicial body. We could relieve it of that power by clarifying those clauses so that their meaning and application is no longer a matter of honest dispute. If we wish to make sure that the power of Congress under the commerce clause includes the regulation of laboring conditions under which goods are made for the interstate market, then let us say so with definiteness and precision. If we are tired of having the due process of law clause used by conservative judges to throttle needed social legislation, let us make clear what we wish the due process limitation to mean, or discard it altogether. I believe we should all be better satisfied if, without impairing the integrity or the traditions of our judicial system, we left to the Court the task of applying constitutional clauses which have reasonably definite meaning, instead of attacking it for giving what we feel is the wrong meaning to clauses so vague as to have no clear and concrete meaning of their own. Our whole judicial system would gain in efficiency, and in public confidence, under such a change. . . .

I have undertaken to show that this power has enabled the Court to dominate wide ranges of legislative policy in the light of the opinions and prejudices of the justices, and I have suggested that this exercise of essentially legislative power by a court of law conflicts with the democratic principle upon which we have built our governmental system. I have no patience with the attitude of constitutional ancestor-worship which rejects as sacrilege any change in the Constitution or in the Supreme Court's power of judicial review, but I have no desire to see the power of judicial review pulled up by the roots or mutilated. Let the Supreme Court clean its own house. Let it replace an arrogantly ruthless attitude toward the exercise by Congress of its legislative discretion, by the tolerant aloofness which bespeaks the judge and not the lawmaker. Let the President and the Senate place on the Supreme Court men who appraise correctly the relation between the Court and Congress. If the Supreme Court cannot or will not do this let us, instead of changing the Court or changing its power of judicial review, change the concrete nature of the job which we give it to do. Let us withdraw from the reach of its interpretation those vast uncharted ranges of discretion which come from vague and general clauses of the Constitution. Let us sharpen and clarify the sections in the construction of which the Court now finds it possible to impose its policy judgments upon the country. By following this course we shall preserve and strengthen the best features of the American system of judicial review of legislation. We shall get rid of its weaknesses and its dangers. The Supreme Court of the United States will become not an obstacle but an aid to the smooth and efficient working of democratic government in a great nation.

Benjamin N. Cardozo: THE NATURE OF THE JUDICIAL PROCESS

THE courts, then, are free in marking the limits of the individual's immunities to shape their judgments in accordance with reason and justice. That does not mean that in judging the validity of statutes they are free to substitute their own ideas of reason and justice for those of the men and women whom they serve. Their standard must be an objective one. In such matters, the thing that counts is not what I believe to be right. It is what I may reasonably believe that some other man of normal intellect and conscience might reasonably look upon as right.

From Benjamin N. Cardozo, *The Nature of the Judicial Process*, Yale University Press, New Haven: 1921, pp. 88–94. Reprinted with the permission of the Yale University Press.

"While the courts must exercise a judgment of their own, it by no means is true that every law is void which may seem to the judges who pass upon it excessive, unsuited to its ostensible end, or based upon conceptions of morality with which they disagree. Considerable latitude must be allowed for difference of view as well as for possible peculiar conditions which this court can know but imperfectly, if at all. Otherwise a constitution, instead of embodying only relatively fundamental rules of right, as generally understood by all English-speaking communities, would become the partisan of a particular set of ethical or economical opinions, which by no means are held *semper ubique et ab omnibus*." Here as so often in the law, "the standard of conduct is external, and takes no account of the personal equation of the man concerned." "The interpreter," says Brutt, "must above all things put aside his estimate of political and legislative values, and must endeavor to ascertain in a purely objective spirit what ordering of the social life of the community comports best with the aim of the law in question in the circumstances before him." Some fields of the law there are, indeed, where there is freer scope for subjective vision. . . . The personal element, whatever its scope in other spheres, should have little, if any sway in determining the limits of legislative power. One department of the government may not force upon another its own standards of propriety. "It must be remembered that legislatures are ultimate guardians of the liberties and welfare of the people in quite as great a degree as courts."

Some critics of our public law insist that the power of the courts to fix the limits of permissible encroachment by statute upon the liberty of the individual is one that ought to be withdrawn. It means, they say, either too much or too little. If it is freely exercised, if it is made an excuse for imposing the individual beliefs and philosophies of the judges upon other branches of the government, if it stereotypes legislation within the forms and limits that were expedient in the nineteenth or perhaps the eighteenth century, it shackles progress, and breeds distrust and suspicion of the courts. If on the other hand, it is interpreted in the broad and variable sense which I believe to be the true one, if statutes are to be sustained unless they are so plainly arbitrary and oppressive that right-minded men and women could not reasonably regard them otherwise, the right of supervision, it is said, is not worth the danger of abuse. "There no doubt comes a time when a statute is so obviously oppressive and absurd that it can have no justification in any sane polity." Such times may indeed come, yet only seldom. The occasions must be few when legislatures will enact a statute that will merit condemnation upon the application of a test so liberal; and if carelessness or haste or momentary passion may at rare intervals bring such statutes into being with hardship to individuals or classes, we may trust to succeeding legislatures for the undoing of the wrong. That is the argument of the critics of the existing system. My own belief is that it lays too little stress on the value of the "imponderables." The utility of an external power restraining the legislative judgment is not to be measured by counting the occasions of its exercise. The great ideals of liberty and equality are preserved against the assaults of opportunism, the expediency of the passing hour, the erosion of small encroachments, the scorn and derision of those who have no patience with general principles, by enshrining them in constitutions, and consecrating to the task of their protection a body of defenders. By conscious or subconscious influence, the presence of this restraining power, aloof in the background, but none the less always in reserve, tends to stabilize and rationalize the legislative judgment, to infuse it with the glow of principle, to hold the standard aloft and visible for those who must run the race and keep the faith. I do not mean to deny that there have been times when the possibility of judicial review has worked the other way. Legislatures have sometimes disregarded their own responsibility, and passed it on to the courts. Such dangers must be balanced against those of independence from all restraint, independence on the part of public officers elected for brief terms, without the guiding force of a continuous tradition. On the whole, I believe the latter dangers to be the more formidable of the two. Great maxims, if they may be violated with impunity, are honored often with lip-service, which passes easily into irreverence. The restraining power of the judiciary does not manifest its chief worth in the few cases in which the legislature has gone beyond the lines that mark the limits of discretion. Rather shall we find its chief worth in making vocal and audible the ideals that might otherwise be silenced, in giving them continuity of life and of expression, in guiding and directing choice within the limits where choice ranges. This function should preserve to the courts the power that now belongs to them, if only the power is exercised with insight into social values, and with suppleness of adaptation to changing social needs.

II. SEGREGATION: THE DECISION

DRED SCOTT *v.* SANDFORD

Mr. Chief Justice Taney delivered the opinion of the court. . . .

THERE are two leading questions presented by the record:

1. Had the Circuit Court of the United States jurisdiction to hear and determine the case between these parties? And

2. If it had jurisdiction, is the judgment it has given erroneous or not?

The plaintiff in error, who was also the plaintiff in the court below, was, with his wife and children, held as a slave by the defendant, in the State of Missouri; and he brought this action in the Circuit Court of the United States for that district, to assert the title of himself and his family to freedom. . . . The question is simply this: Can a negro, whose ancestors were imported into this country, and sold as slaves, become a member of the political community formed and brought into existence by the Constitution of the United States, and as such become entitled to all the rights, and privileges, and immunities, guaranteed by that instrument to the citizen? One of which rights is the privilege of suing in a court of the United States in the cases specified in the Constitution. . . . We think they are not, and that they are not included, and were not intended to be included, under the word "citizens" in the Constitution, and can therefore claim none of the rights and privileges which that instrument provides for and secures to citizens of the United States. On the contrary, they were at that time considered as a subordinate and inferior class of beings, who had been subjugated by the dominant race, and, whether emancipated or not, yet remained subject to their authority, and had no rights or privileges but such as those who held the power and the Government might choose to grant them. . . .

In the opinion of the court, the legislation and histories of the times, and the language used in the Declaration of Independence, show, that neither the class of persons who had been imported as slaves, nor their descendants, whether they had become free or not, were then acknowledged as a part of the people, nor intended to be included in the general words used in that memorable instrument. . . . They had for more than a century before been regarded as beings of an inferior order, and altogether unfit to associate with the white race, either in social or political relations; and so far inferior, that they had no rights which the white man was bound to respect; and that the negro might justly and lawfully be reduced to slavery for his benefit. He was bought and sold, and treated as an ordinary article of merchandise and traffic, whenever a profit could be made by it. This opinion was at that time fixed and universal in the civilized portion of the white race. It was regarded as an axiom in morals as well as in politics, which no one thought of disputing, or

19 Howard 393 (1856)

supposed to be open to dispute; and men in every grade and position in society daily and habitually acted upon it in their private pursuits, as well as in matters of public concern, without doubting for a moment the correctness of this opinion. . . .

The language of the Declaration of Independence is equally conclusive:

It begins by declaring that, "when in the course of human events it becomes necessary for one people to dissolve the political bands which have connected them with another, and to assume among the powers of the earth the separate and equal station to which the laws of nature and nature's God entitle them, a decent respect for the opinions of mankind requires that they should declare the causes which impel them to the separation."

It then proceeds to say: "We hold these truths to be self-evident: that all men are created equal; that they are endowed by their Creator with certain unalienable rights; that among these are life, liberty, and the pursuit of happiness. That, to secure these rights, Governments are instituted among men, deriving their just powers from the consent of the governed."

The general words above quoted would seem to embrace the whole human family, and if they were used in a similar instrument at this day would be so understood. But it is too clear for dispute, that the enslaved African race were not intended to be included, and formed no part of the people who framed and adopted this declaration; for if the language, as understood in that day, would embrace them, the conduct of the distinguished men who framed the Declaration of Independence would have been utterly and flagrantly inconsistent with the principles they asserted; and instead of the sympathy of mankind, to which they so confidently appealed, they would have deserved and received universal rebuke and reprobation. . . . This state of public opinion had undergone no change when the Constitution was adopted, as is equally evident from its provisions and language. . . . But there are two clauses in the Constitution which point directly and specifically to the negro race as a separate class of persons and shows clearly that they were not regarded as a portion of the people or citizens of the Government then formed.

One of these clauses reserves to each of the thirteen States the right to import slaves until the year 1808, if it thinks proper. And the importation which it thus sanctions was unquestionably of persons of the race of which we are speaking, as the traffic in slaves in the United States had always been confined to them. And by the other provision the States pledge themselves to each other to maintain the right of property of the master, by delivering up to him any slave who may have escaped from his service, and be found within their respective territories. By the first above-mentioned clause, therefore, the right to purchase and hold this property is directly sanctioned and authorized for twenty years by the people who framed the Constitution. And by the second, they pledge themselves to maintain and uphold the right of the master in the manner specified, as long as the Government they then formed should endure. And these two provisions show, conclusively, that neither the description of persons therein referred to, nor their descendants, were embraced in any of the other provisions of the Constitution; for certainly these two clauses were not intended to confer on them or their posterity the blessings of liberty, or any of the personal rights so carefully provided for the citizen. . . .

It is very true, that in that portion of the Union where the labor of the negro race was found to be unsuited to the climate and unprofitable to the master, but few slaves were held at the time of the Declaration of Independence; and when the Constitution was adopted, it had entirely worn out in one of them, and measures had been taken for its gradual abolition in several others. But this change had not been produced by any change of opinion in relation to this race; but because it was discovered, from experience, that slave labor was unsuited to the climate and productions of these States: for some of the States, where it had ceased or nearly ceased to exist, were actively engaged in the slave trade, procuring cargoes on the coast of Africa, and transporting them for sale to those parts of the Union where their labor was found to be profitable, and suited to the climate and productions. And this traffic was openly carried on, and fortunes accumulated by it, without reproach from the people of the States where they resided. And it can hardly be supposed that, in the States where it was then countenanced in its worst form—that is, in the seizure and transportation—the people could have regarded those who were emancipated as entitled to equal rights with themselves. . . .

The legislation of the States therefore shows, in a manner not to be mistaken, the inferior and subject condition of that race at the time the Constitution was adopted, and long afterwards, throughout the thirteen States by which that instrument was framed; and it is hardly consistent with the respect due to these States, to suppose that they regarded at that time, as fellow-citizens and members of the sovereignty, a class of beings whom they had thus stigmatized; whom, as we are bound, out of respect to the State sovereignties, to assume they had deemed it just and necessary thus to stigmatize, and upon whom they had impressed such deep and enduring marks of inferiority and degradation; or, that when they met in convention to form the Constitution, they looked upon them as a portion of their constituents, or designed to include them in the provisions so carefully inserted for the security and protection of the liberties and rights of their citizens. It cannot be supposed that they intended to secure to them rights, and privileges, and rank, in the new political body throughout the Union, which every one of them denied within the limits of its own dominion. More especially, it cannot be believed that the large slaveholding States regarded them as included in the word citizens, or would have consented to a Constitution which might compel them to receive them in that character from another State. . . .

To all this mass of proof we have still to add, that Congress has repeatedly legislated upon the same construction of the Constitution that we have given. Three laws, two of which were passed almost immediately after the Government went into operation, will be abundantly sufficient to show this. The two first are particularly worthy of notice, because many of the men who assisted in framing the Constitution, and took an active part in procuring its adoption, were then in the halls of legislation, and certainly understood what they meant when they used the words "people of the United States" and "citizen" in that well-considered instrument.

The first of these acts is the naturalization law, which was passed at the second session of the first Congress, March 26, 1790, and confines the right of becoming citizens *"to aliens being free white persons."*

Now, the Constitution does not limit the power of Congress in this respect to white persons. And they may, if they think proper, authorize the naturalization of any one, of any color, who was born under allegiance to another Government. . . . Another of the early laws of which we have spoken, is the first militia law, which was passed in 1792, at the first session of the second Congress. The language of this law is equally plain and significant with the one just mentioned. It directs that every "free able-bodied white male citizen" shall be enrolled in the militia. . . . The third act to which we have alluded is even still more decisive; it was passed as late as 1813, (2 Stat., 809,) and it provides: "That from and after the termination of the war in which the United States are now engaged with Great Britain, it shall not be lawful to employ, on board of any public or private vessels of the United States, any person or persons except citizens of the United States, *or* persons of color, natives of the United States.". . .

The conduct of the Executive Department of the Government has been in perfect harmony upon this subject with this course of legislation. The question was brought officially before the late William Wirt, when he was the Attorney General of the United States, in 1821, and he decided that the words "citizens of the United States" were used in the acts of Congress in the same sense as in the Constitution; and that free persons of color were not citizens, within the meaning of the Constitution and laws; and this opinion has been confirmed by that of the late Attorney General, Caleb Cushing, in a recent case, and acted upon by the Secretary of State, who refused to grant passports to them as "citizens of the United States.". . . No one, we presume, supposes that any change in public opinion or feeling, in relation to this unfortunate race, in the civilized nations of Europe or in this country, should induce the court to give to the words of the Constitution a more liberal construction in their favor than they were intended to bear when the instrument was framed and adopted. Such an argument would be altogether inadmissible in any tribunal called on to interpret it. If any of its provisions are deemed unjust, there is a mode prescribed in the instrument itself by which it may be amended; but while it remains unaltered, it must be construed now as it was understood at the time of its adoption. It is not only the same in words, but the same in meaning, and delegates the same powers to the Government, and reserves and secures the same rights and privileges to the citizen; and as long as it continues to exist in its present form, it speaks not only in the same words, but with the same meaning and intent with which it spoke when it came from the hands of its framers, and was voted on and adopted by the people of the United States. Any other rule of construction would abrogate the judicial character of this court, and make it the mere reflex of the popular opinion or passion of the day. This court was not created by the Constitution for such purposes. Higher and graver trusts have been confided to it, and it must not falter in the path of duty.

What the construction was at that time, we think can hardly admit of doubt. We have the language of the Declaration of Independence and of the Articles of Confederation, in addition to plain words of the Constitution itself; we have the legislation of the different States, before, about the time, and since, the Constitution was adopted; we have the legislation of Congress, from the time of its adoption to a recent period; and we have the constant and uniform action of the Executive Department, all concurring together, and leading to the same result. And if anything in relation to the construction of the Constitution can be regarded as settled, it is that which we now give to the word "citizen" and the word "people."

And upon a full and careful consideration of the subject, the court is of opinion, that, upon the facts stated in the plea in abatement, Dred Scott was not a citizen of Missouri within the meaning of the Constitution of the United States, and not entitled as such to sue in its courts; and, consequently, that the Circuit Court had no jurisdiction of the case, and that the judgment on the plea in abatement is erroneous. . . .

We proceed, therefore, to inquire whether the facts relied on by the plaintiff entitled him to his freedom. . . .

The act of Congress, upon which the plaintiff relies, declares that slavery and involuntary servitude, except as a punishment for crime, shall be forever prohibited in all that part of the territory ceded by France, under the name of Louisiana, which lies north of thirty-six degrees thirty minutes north latitude, and not included within the limits of Missouri. And the difficulty which meets us at the threshold of this part of the inquiry is, whether Congress was authorized to pass this law under any of the powers granted to it by the Constitution; for if the authority is not given by that instrument, it is the duty of this court to declare it void and inoperative, and incapable of conferring freedom upon any one who is held as a slave under the laws of any one of the States. . . .

But the power of Congress over the person or property of a citizen can never be a mere discretionary power under our Constitution and form of Government. The powers of the Government and the rights and privileges of the citizen are regulated and plainly defined by the Constitution itself. And when the Territory becomes a part of the United States, the Federal Government enters into possession in the character impressed upon it by those who created it. It enters upon it with its powers over the citizen strictly defined, and limited by the Constitution, from which it derives its own existence, and by virtue of which alone it continues to exist and act as a Government and sovereignty. It has no power of any kind beyond it; and it cannot, when it enters a Territory of the United States, put off its character, and assume discretionary or despotic powers which the Constitution has denied to it. It cannot create for itself a new character separated from the citizens of the United States, and the duties it owes them under the provisions of the Constitution. The Territory being a part of the United States, the Government and the citizen both enter it under the authority of the Constitution, with their respective rights defined and marked out; and the Federal Government can exercise no power over his person or property, beyond what that instrument confers, nor lawfully deny any right which it has reserved. . . .

Now, as we have already said in an earlier part of this opinion, upon a different point, the right of property in a slave is distinctly and expressly affirmed in the Constitution. The right to traffic in it, like an ordinary article of merchandise and property, was guaranteed to the citizens of the United States, in every State that might desire it, for twenty years. And the Government in express terms is pledged to protect it in all future time, if the slave escapes from his owner. This is done in plain words – too plain to be misunderstood. And no word can be found in the Constitution which gives Congress a greater power over slave property, or which entitles property of that kind to less protection than property of any other description. The only power conferred is the power coupled with the duty of guarding and protecting the owner in his rights.

Upon these considerations, it is the opinion of the court that the act of Congress which prohibited a citizen from holding and owning property of this kind in the territory of the United States north of the line therein mentioned, is not warranted by the Constitution, and is therefore void; and that neither Dred Scott himself, nor any of his family, were made free by being carried into this territory; even if they had been carried there by the owner, with the intention of becoming a permanent resident. . . .

From the CONSTITUTION OF THE UNITED STATES

AMENDMENT XIII
(December 18, 1865)

SECTION 1. Neither slavery nor involuntary servitude, except as a punishment for crime whereof the party shall have been duly convicted, shall exist within the United States, or any place subject to their jurisdiction.

SECTION 2. Congress shall have power to enforce this article by appropriate legislation.

AMENDMENT XIV
(July 28, 1868)

SECTION 1. All persons born or naturalized in the United States, and subject to the jurisdiction thereof, are citizens of the United States and of the State wherein they reside. No State shall make or enforce any law which shall abridge the privileges or immunities of citizens of the United States; nor shall any State deprive any person of life, liberty, or property, without due process of law; nor deny to any person within its jurisdiction the equal protection of the laws.

SECTION 2. Representatives shall be apportioned among the several States according to their respective numbers, counting the whole number of persons in each State, excluding Indians not taxed. But when the right to vote at any election for the choice of electors for President and Vice-President of the United States, Representatives in Congress, the executive and judicial officers of a State, or the members of the legislature thereof, is denied to any of the male inhabitants of such State, being twenty-one years of age, and citizens of the United States, or in any way abridged, except for participation in rebellion, or other crime, the basis of representation therein shall be reduced in the proportion which the number of such male citizens shall bear to the whole number of male citizens twenty-one years of age in such State.

SECTION 3. No person shall be a Senator or Representative in Congress, or elector of President and Vice-President, or hold any office, civil or military under the United States or under any State, who, having previously taken an oath as a member of Congress, or as an officer of the United States, or as a member of any State legislature, or as an executive or judicial officer of any State, to support the Constitution of the United States, shall have engaged in insurrection or rebellion against the same, or given aid or comfort to the enemies thereof. But Congress may, by a vote of two thirds of each house, remove such disability.

SECTION 4. The validity of the public debt of the United States, authorized by law, including debts incurred for payment of pensions and bounties for services in suppressing insurrection or rebellion, shall not be questioned. But neither the United States nor any State shall assume or pay any debt or obligation incurred in aid of insurrection or rebellion against the United States, or any claim for the loss or emancipation of any slave; but all such debts, obligations, and claims shall be held illegal and void.

SECTION 5. The Congress shall have power to enforce, by appropriate legislation, the provisions of this article.

CIVIL RIGHTS CASES

Mr. Justice Bradley delivered the opinion of the court. . . .

IT is obvious that the primary and important question in all the cases is the constitutionality of the law: for if the law is unconstitutional none of the prosecutions can stand. . . .

Sec. 1. That all persons within the jurisdiction of the United States shall be entitled to the full and equal enjoyment of the accommodations, advantages, facilities, and privileges of inns, public conveyances on land or water, theatres, and other places of public amusement; subject only to the conditions and limitations established by law, and applicable alike to citizens of every race and color, regardless of any previous condition of servitude. . . .

In other words, it is the purpose of the law to declare that, in the enjoyment of the accommodations and privileges of inns, public conveyances, theatres, and other places of public amusement, no distinction shall be made between citizens of different race or color, or between those who have, and those who have not, been slaves. Its effect is to declare, that in all inns, public conveyances, and places of amusement, colored citizens, whether formerly slaves or not, and citizens of other races shall have the same accommodations and privileges in all inns, public conveyances, and places of amusement as are enjoyed by white citizens, and *vice versa*. . . .

Has Congress constitutional power to make such a law? Of course, no one will contend that the power to pass it was contained in the Constitution before the adoption of the last three amendments. The power is sought, first, in the Fourteenth Amendment, and the views and arguments of distinguished Senators, advanced whilst the law was under consideration, claiming authority to pass it by virtue of that amendment, are the principal arguments adduced in favor of the power. We have carefully considered those arguments, as was due to the eminent ability of those who put them forward, and have felt, in all its force, the weight of authority which always invests a law that Congress deems itself competent to pass. But the responsibility of an independent judgment is now thrown upon this court; and we are bound to exercise it according to the best lights we have.

The first section of the Fourteenth

109 U.S. 3 (1883)

Amendment (which is the one relied on), after declaring who shall be citizens of the United States, and of the several States, is prohibitory in its character, and prohibitory upon the States. It declares that:

> No State shall make or enforce any law which shall abridge the privileges or immunities of citizens of the United States; nor shall any State deprive any person of life, liberty, or property without due process of law; nor deny to any person within its jurisdiction the equal protection of the laws.

It is State action of a particular character that is prohibited. Individual invasion of individual rights is not the subject-matter of the amendment. It has a deeper and broader scope. It nullifies and makes void all State legislation, and State action of every kind, which impairs the privileges and immunities of citizens of the United States, or which injures them in life, liberty or property without due process of law, or which denies to any of them the equal protection of the laws. It not only does this, but, in order that the national will, thus declared, may not be a mere *brutum fulmen,* the last section of the amendment invests Congress with power to enforce it by appropriate legislation. To enforce what? To enforce the prohibition. To adopt appropriate legislation for correcting the effects of such prohibited State laws and State acts, and thus to render them effectually null, void, and innocuous. This is the legislative power conferred upon Congress, and this is the whole of it. It does not invest Congress with power to legislate upon subjects which are within the domain of State legislation; but to provide modes of relief against State legislation, or State action, of the kind referred to. It does not authorize Congress to create a code of municipal law for the regulation of private rights; but to provide modes of redress against the operation of State laws and the action of State officers, executive or judicial, when these are subversive of the fundamental rights specified in the amendment. Positive rights and privileges are undoubtedly secured by the Fourteenth Amendment; but they are secured by way of prohibition against State laws and State proceedings affecting those rights and privileges, and by power given to Congress to legislate for the purpose of carrying such prohibition into effect: and such legislation must necessarily be predicated upon such supposed State laws or State proceedings, and be directed to the correction of their operation and effect. . . .

And so in the present case, until some State law has been passed, or some State action through its officers or agents has been taken, adverse to the rights of citizens sought to be protected by the Fourteenth Amendment, no legislation of the United States under said amendment, nor any proceeding under such legislation, can be called into activity; for the prohibitions of the amendment are against State laws and acts done under State authority. Of course, legislation may, and should be, provided in advance to meet the exigency when it arises; but it should be adapted to the mischief and wrong which the amendment was intended to provide against; and that is, State laws, or State action of some kind, adverse to the rights of the citizen secured by the amendment. Such legislation cannot properly cover the whole domain of rights appertaining to life, liberty and property, defining them and providing for their vindication. That would be to establish a code of municipal law regulative of all private rights between man and man in society. It would be to make Congress take the place of the State legislatures and to supersede them. It is absurd to affirm that, because the rights of life, liberty and property (which include all civil rights that men have), are by the amendment sought to be protected against invasion on the part of the State without due process of law, Congress may therefore, provide due process of law for their vindication in every case; and that, because the denial by a State to any persons, of the equal protection of the laws, is prohibited by the amendment, therefore Congress may establish laws for their equal protection. In fine, the legislation which Congress is authorized to adopt in this behalf is not general legislation upon the rights of the citizen, but corrective legislation, that is, such as may be necessary and proper for counteracting such laws as the States may adopt or enforce, and which, by the amendment, they are prohibited from making or enforcing, or such acts and proceedings as the States may commit or take, and which, by the amendment, they are prohibited from committing or taking. It is not necessary for us to state, if we could, what legislation would be proper for Congress to adopt. It is sufficient for us to examine whether the law in question is of that character.

An inspection of the law shows that it makes no reference whatever to any supposed or apprehended violation of the Fourteenth Amendment on the part of the States. It is not predicated on any such view. It proceeds *ex directo* to declare that certain acts committed by individuals shall be deemed offences, and shall be prosecuted and punished by proceedings in the courts of the United States. It does not profess to be corrective of any constitutional wrong committed by the States; it does not make its operation to depend upon any such wrong committed. It applies equally to cases arising in States which have the justest laws respecting the personal rights of citizens, and whose authorities are ever ready to enforce such laws, as to those which arise in States that may have violated the prohibition of the amendment. In other words, it steps into the domain of local jurisprudence, and lays down rules for the conduct of individuals in society towards each other, and imposes sanctions for the enforcement of those rules, without referring in any manner to any supposed action of the State or its authorities.

If this legislation is appropriate for enforcing the prohibitions of the amendment, it is difficult to see where it is to stop. Why may not Congress with equal show of authority enact a code of laws for the enforcement and vindication of all rights of life, liberty, and property? If it is supposable that the States may deprive persons of life, liberty, and property without due process of law (and the amendment itself does suppose this), why should not Congress proceed at once to prescribe due process of law for the protection of every one of these fundamental rights, in every possible case, as well as to prescribe equal privileges in inns, public conveyances, and theatres? The truth is, that the implication of a power to legislate in this manner is based upon the assumption that if the States are forbidden to legislate or act in a particular way on a particular subject, and power is conferred upon Congress to enforce the prohibition, this gives Congress power to legislate generally upon that subject, and not merely power to provide modes of redress against such State legislation or action. The assumption is certainly unsound. It is repugnant to the Tenth Amendment of the Constitution, which declares that powers not delegated to the United States by the Constitution, nor prohibited by it to the States, are reserved to the States respectively or to the people. . . .

If the principles of interpretation which we have laid down are correct, as we deem them to be . . . it is clear that the law in question cannot be sustained by any grant of legislative power made to Congress by the Fourteenth Amendment. That amendment prohibits the States from denying to any person the equal protection of the laws, and declares that Congress shall have power to enforce, by appropriate legislation, the provisions of the amendment. The law in question, without any reference to adverse State legislation on the subject, declares that all persons shall be entitled to equal accommodations and privileges of inns, public conveyances, and places of public amusement, and imposes a penalty upon any individual who shall deny to any citizen such equal accommodations and privileges. This is not corrective legislation; it is primary and direct; it takes immediate and absolute possession of the subject of the right of admission to inns, public conveyances, and places of amusement. It supersedes and displaces State legislation on the same subject, or only allows it permissive force. It ignores such legislation, and assumes that the matter is one that belongs to the domain of national regulation. Whether it would not have been a more effective protection of the rights of citizens to have clothed Congress with plenary power over the whole subject, is not now the question. What we have to decide is, whether such plenary power has been conferred upon Congress by the Fourteenth Amendment; and, in our judgment, it has not. . . .

Conceding the major proposition to be true, that Congress has a right to enact all necessary and proper laws for the obliteration and prevention of slavery with all its badges and incidents, is the minor proposition also true, that the denial to any person of admission to the accommodations and privileges of an inn, a public conveyance, or a theatre, does subject that person to any form of servitude, or tend to fasten upon him any badge of slavery? If it does not, then power to pass the law is not found in the Thirteenth Amendment. . . .

After giving to these questions all the consideration which their importance demands, we are forced to the conclusion that such an act of refusal has nothing to do with slavery or involuntary servitude, and that if it is violative of any right of the party, his redress is to be sought under the laws of the State; or if those laws are adverse to his rights and do not protect him, his remedy will be found in the corrective legislation which Congress has adopted, or may adopt, for counteracting the effect of State laws, or State action, prohibited by the Fourteenth Amendment. It would be running the slavery argument into the ground to make it apply to every act of discrimination which a person may see fit to make as to the guests he will entertain, or as to the people he will take into his coach or cab or car, or admit to his concert or theatre, or deal with in other matters of intercourse or business. . . .

On the whole we are of opinion, that no countenance of authority for the passage of the law in question can be found in either the Thirteenth or Fourteenth Amendment of the Constitution; and no other ground of authority for its passage being suggested, it must necessarily be declared void, at least so far as its operation in the several States is concerned. . . .

Mr. Justice Harlan dissenting

The opinion in these cases proceeds, it seems to me, upon ground entirely too narrow and artificial. I cannot resist the conclusion that the substance and spirit of the recent amendments of the Constitution have been sacrificed by a subtle and ingenious verbal criticism. "It is not the words of the law but the internal sense of it that makes the law; the letter of the law is the body; the sense and reason of the law is the soul." Constitutional provisions, adopted in the interest of liberty, and for the purpose of securing, through national legislation, if need be, rights inhering in a state of freedom, and belonging to American citizenship, have been so construed as to defeat the ends the people desired to accomplish, which they attempted to accomplish, and which they supposed they had accomplished by changes in their fundamental law. By this I do not mean that the determination of these cases should have been materially controlled by considerations of mere expediency or policy. I mean only, in this form, to express an earnest conviction that the court has departed from the familiar rule requiring, in the interpretation of constitutional provisions, that full effect be given to the intent with which they were adopted. . . .

The court adjudges, I think erroneously, that Congress is without power, under either the Thirteenth or Fourteenth Amendment, to establish such regulations, and that the first and second sections of the statute are, in all their parts, unconstitutional and void.

Whether the legislative department of the government has transcended the limits of its constitutional powers, "is at all times," said this court in *Fletcher v. Peck,* 6 Cr. 128, "a question of much delicacy, which ought seldom, if ever, to be decided in the affirmative, in a doubtful case. . . . The opposition between the Constitution and the law should be such that the judge feels a clear and strong conviction of their incompatibility with each other." More recently in *Sinking Fund Cases,* 99 U. S., 718, we said: "It is our duty when required in the regular course of judicial proceedings, to declare an act of Congress void if not within the legislative power of the United States, but this declaration should never be made except in a clear case. Every possible presumption is in favor of the validity of a statute, and this continues until the contrary is shown beyond a rational doubt. One branch of the government cannot encroach on the domain of another without danger. The safety of our institutions depends in no small degree on a strict observance of this salutary rule." . . .

The Fourteenth Amendment presents the first instance in our history of the investiture of Congress with affirmative power by *legislation,* to *enforce* an express prohibition upon the States. It is not said that the *judicial* power of the nation may be exerted for the enforcement of that amendment. No enlargement of the judicial power was required, for it is clear that had the fifth section of the Fourteenth Amendment been entirely omitted, the judiciary could have stricken down all State laws and nullified all State proceedings in hostility to rights and privileges secured or recognized by that amendment. The power given is, in terms, by congressional *legislation,* to enforce the provisions of the amendment. . . .

This court has always given a broad and liberal construction to the Constitution, so as to enable Congress, by legislation, to enforce rights secured by that instrument. The legislation which Congress may enact, in execution of its power to enforce the provisions of this amendment, is such as may be appropriate to protect the right granted. The word appropriate was undoubtedly used with reference to its meaning, as established by repeated decisions of this court. Under given circumstances, that which the court characterizes as corrective legislation might be deemed by Congress appropriate and entirely sufficient. Under other circumstances primary direct legislation may be required. But it is for Congress, not the judiciary, to say that legislation is appropriate – that is – best adapted to the end to be attained. The judiciary may not, with safety to our institution, enter the domain of legislative discretion, and dictate the means which Congress shall employ in the exercise of its granted powers. That would be sheer usurpation of the functions of a co-ordinate department, which, if often repeated, and permanently acquiesced in, would work a radical change in our system of government. . . .

With all respect for the opinion of others, I insist that the national legislature may, without transcending the limits of the Constitution, do for human liberty and the fundamental rights of American citizenship, what it did, with the sanction of this court, for the protection of slavery and the rights of the masters of fugitive slaves. If fugitive slave laws, providing modes and prescribing penalties, whereby the master could seize and recover his fugitive slave, were legitimate exercises of an implied power to protect and enforce a right recognized by the Constitution, why shall the hands of Congress be tied, so that – under an express power, by appropriate legislation, to enforce a constitutional provision granting citizenship – it may not, by means of direct legislation, bring the whole power of this nation to bear upon States and their officers, and upon such individuals and corporations exercising public functions as assume to abridge, impair, or deny rights confessedly secured by the supreme law of the land? . . . .

It was said of the case of *Dred Scott v. Sandford,* that this court, there overruled the action of two generations, virtually inserted a new clause in the Constitution, changed its character, and made a new departure in the workings of the federal government. I may be permitted to say that if the recent amendments are so construed that Congress may not, in its own discretion, and independently of the action or nonaction of the States, provide, by legislation of a direct character, for the security of rights created by the national Constitution; if it be adjudged that the obligation to protect the fundamental privileges and immunities granted by the Fourteenth Amendment to citizens residing in the several States rests primarily, not on the nation, but on the States; if it be further adjudged that individuals and corporations, exercising public functions, or wielding power under public authority, may, without liability to direct primary legislation on the part of Congress, make the race of citizens the ground for denying them that equality of civil rights which the Constitution ordains as a principle of republican citizenship; then, not only the foundations upon which the national supremacy has always securely rested will be materially disturbed, but we shall enter upon an era of constitutional law, when the rights of freedom and American citizenship cannot receive from the nation that efficient protection which heretofore was unhesitatingly accorded to slavery and the rights of the master. . . .

What the nation, through the Congress, has sought to accomplish in reference to that race, is — what had already been done in every State of the Union for the white race — to secure and protect rights belonging to them as freemen and citizens; nothing more. It was not deemed enough "to help the feeble up, but to support him after." The one underlying purpose of congressional legislation has been to enable the black race to take the rank of mere citizens. The difficulty has been to compel a recognition of the legal right of the black race to take the rank of citizens, and to secure the enjoyment of privileges belonging, under the law, to them as a component part of the people for whose welfare and happiness government is ordained. At every step, in this direction, the nation has been confronted with class tyranny, which a contemporary English historian says is, of all tyrannies, the most intolerable, "for it is ubiquitous in its operation, and weighs, perhaps, most heavily on those whose obscurity or distance would withdraw them from the notice of a single despot." To-day, it is the colored race which is denied, by corporations and individuals wielding public authority, rights fundamental in their freedom and citizenship. At some future time, it may be that some other race will fall under the ban of race discrimination. If the constitutional amendments be enforced, according to the intent with which, as I conceive, they were adopted, there cannot be, in this republic, any class of human beings in practical subjection to another class, with power in the latter to dole out to the former just such privileges as they may choose to grant. The supreme law of the land has decreed that no authority shall be exercised in this country upon the basis of discrimination, in respect of civil rights, against freemen and citizens because of their race, color, or previous condition of servitude. To that decree — for the due enforcement of which, by appropriate legislation, Congress has been invested with express power — every one must bow, whatever may have been, or whatever now are, his individual views as to the wisdom or policy, either of the recent changes in the fundamental law, or of the legislation which has been enacted to give them effect. . . .

PLESSY *v.* FERGUSON

Mr. Justice Brown delivered the opinion of the court.

THIS case turns upon the constitutionality of an act of the General Assembly of the State of Louisiana, passed in 1890, providing for separate railway carriages for the white and colored races. Acts 1890, No. 111, p. 152.

The first section of the statute enacts "that all railway companies carrying passengers in their coaches in this State, shall provide equal but separate accommodations for the white, and colored races, by providing two or more passenger coaches for each passenger train, or by dividing the passenger coaches by a partition so as to secure separate accommodations: *Provided*, That this section shall not be construed to apply to street railroads. No person or persons, shall be admitted to occupy seats in coaches, other than the ones assigned to them, on account of the race they belong to."

By the second section it was enacted

163 U.S. 537 [1895]

"that the officers of such passenger trains shall have power and are hereby required to assign each passenger to the coach or compartment used for the race to which such passenger belongs; any passenger insisting on going into a coach or compartment to which by race he does not belong, shall be liable to a fine of twenty-five dollars, or in lieu thereof to imprisonment for a period of not more than twenty days in the parish prison, and any officer of any railroad insisting on assigning a passenger to a coach or compartment other than the one set aside for the race to which said passenger belongs, shall be liable to a fine of twenty-five dollars, or in lieu thereof to imprisonment for a period of not more than twenty days in the parish prison; and should any passenger refuse to occupy the coach or compartment to which he or she is assigned by the officer of such railway, said officer shall have power to refuse to carry such passenger on his train, and for such refusal neither he nor the railway company which he represents shall be liable for damages in any of the courts of this State."

The third section provides penalties for the refusal or neglect of the officers, directors, conductors and employés of railway companies to comply with the act, with a proviso that "nothing in this act shall be construed as applying to nurses attending children of the other race." The fourth section is immaterial.

The information filed in the criminal District Court charged in substance that Plessy, being a passenger between two stations within the State of Louisiana, was assigned by officers of the company to the coach used for the race to which he belonged, but he insisted upon going into a coach used by the race to which he did not belong. Neither in the information nor plea was his particular race or color averred.

The petition for the writ of prohibition averred that petitioner was seven eighths Caucasian and one eighth African blood; that the mixture of colored blood was not discernible in him, and that he was entitled to every right, privilege and immunity secured to citizens of the United States of the white race; and that, upon such theory, he took possession of a vacant seat in a coach where passengers of the white race were accommodated, and was ordered by the conductor to vacate said coach and take a seat in another assigned to persons of the colored race, and having refused to comply with such demand he was forcibly ejected with the aid of a police officer, and imprisoned in the parish jail to answer a charge of having violated the above act.

The constitutionality of this act is attacked upon the ground that it conflicts both with the Thirteenth Amendment of the Constitution, abolishing slavery, and the Fourteenth Amendment, which prohibits certain restrictive legislation on the part of the States.

1. That it does not conflict with the Thirteenth Amendment, which abolished slavery and involuntary servitude, except as a punishment for crime, is too clear for argument. Slavery implies involuntary servitude – a state of bondage; the ownership of mankind as a chattel, or at least the control of the labor and services of one man for the benefit of another, and the absence of a legal right to the disposal of his own person, property and services. This amendment was said in the *Slaughter House Cases*, 16 Wall. 36, to have been intended primarily to abolish slavery, as it had been previously known in this country, and that it equally forbade Mexican peonage or the Chinese

coolie trade, when they amounted to slavery or involuntary servitude, and that the use of the word "servitude" was intended to prohibit the use of all forms of involuntary slavery, of whatever class or name. It was intimated, however, in that case that this amendment was regarded by the statesmen of that day as insufficient to protect the colored race from certain laws which had been enacted in the Southern States, imposing upon the colored race onerous disabilities and burdens, and curtailing their rights in the pursuit of life, liberty and property to such an extent that their freedom was of little value; and that the Fourteenth Amendment was devised to meet this exigency.

So, too, in the *Civil Rights Cases,* 109 U.S. 3, it was said that the act of a mere individual, the owner of an inn, a public conveyance or place of amusement, refusing accommodations to colored people, cannot be justly regarded as imposing any badge of slavery or servitude upon the applicant, but only as involving an ordinary civil injury, properly cognizable by the laws of the State, and presumably subject to redress by those laws until the contrary appears. "It would be running the slavery argument into the ground," said Mr. Justice Bradley, "to make it apply to every act of discrimination which a person may see fit to make as to the guests he will entertain, or as to the people he will take into his coach or cab or car, or admit to his concert or theatre, or deal with in other matters of intercourse or business."

A statute which implies merely a legal distinction between the white and colored races — a distinction which is founded in the color of the two races, and which must always exist so long as white men are distinguished from the other race by color — has no tendency to destroy the legal equality of the two races, or reëstablish a state of involuntary servitude. Indeed, we do not understand that the Thirteenth Amendment is strenuously relied upon by the plaintiff in error in this connection.

2. By the Fourteenth Amendment, all persons born or naturalized in the United States, and subject to the jurisdiction thereof, are made citizens of the United States and of the State wherein they reside; and the States are forbidden from making or enforcing any law which shall abridge the privileges or immunities of citizens of the United States, or shall deprive any person of life, liberty or property without due process of law, or deny to any person within their jurisdiction the equal protection of the laws.

The proper construction of this amendment was first called to the attention of this court in the *Slaughter House Cases,* 16 Wall. 36, which involved, however, not a question of race, but one of exclusive privileges. The cases did not call for any expression of opinion as to the exact rights it was intended to secure to the colored race, but it was said generally that its main purpose was to establish the citizenship of the negro; to give definitions of citizenship of the United States and of the States, and to protect from the hostile legislation of the States the privileges and immunities of citizens of the United States, as distinguished from those of citizens of the States.

The object of the amendment was undoubtedly to enforce the absolute equality of the two races before the law, but in the nature of things it could not have been intended to abolish distinctions based upon color, or to enforce social, as distinguished from political equality, or a commingling of the two races upon terms unsatisfactory to either. Laws permitting, and even requiring, their separation in places where they are liable to be brought into contact do not necessarily imply the inferiority of either race to the other, and have been generally, if not universally, recognized as within the competency of the state legislatures in the exercise of their police power. The most common instance of this is connected with the establishment of separate schools for white and colored children, which has been held to be a valid exercise of the legislative power even by courts of States where the political rights of the colored race have been longest and most earnestly enforced.

One of the earliest of these cases is that of *Roberts v. City of Boston,* 5 Cush. 198, in which the Supreme Judicial Court of Massachusetts held that the general school committee of Boston had power to make provision for the instruction of colored children in separate schools established exclusively for them, and to prohibit their attendance upon the other schools. "The great principle," said Chief Justice Shaw, p. 206, "advanced by the learned and eloquent advocate for the the plaintiff," (Mr. Charles Sumner,) "is, that by the constitution and laws of Massachusetts, all persons without distinction of age or sex, birth or color, origin or condition, are equal before the law. . . . But, when this great principle comes to be applied to the actual and various conditions of persons in society, it will not warrant the assertion, that men and women are legally clothed with the same civil and political powers, and that children and adults are legally to have the same functions and be subject to the same treatment; but only that the rights of all, as they are settled and regulated by law, are equally entitled to the paternal consideration and protection of the law for their maintenance and security." It was held that the powers of the committee extended to the establishment of separate schools for children of different ages, sexes and colors, and that they might also establish special schools for poor and neglected children, who have become too old to attend the primary school, and yet have not acquired the rudiments of learning, to enable them to enter the ordinary schools. Similar laws have been enacted by Congress under its general power of legislation over the District of Columbia, Rev. Stat. D.C. Sections 281, 282, 283, 310, 319, as well as by the legislatures of many of the States, and have been generally, if not uniformly, sustained by the courts.

Laws forbidding the intermarriage of the two races may be said in a technical sense to interfere with the freedom of contract, and yet have been universally recognized as within the police power of the State. *State v. Gibson,* 36 Indiana, 389.

The distinction between laws interfering with the political equality of the negro and those requiring the separation of the two races in schools, theatres and railway carriages has been frequently drawn by this court. Thus in *Strauder v. West Virginia,* 100 U.S. 303, it was held that a law of West Virginia limiting to white male persons, 21 years of age and citizens of the State, the right to sit upon juries, was a discrimination which implied a legal inferiority in civil society, which lessened the security of the right of the colored race, and was a step toward reducing them to a condition of servility. Indeed, the right of a colored man that, in the selection of jurors to pass upon his life, liberty and property, there shall be no exclusion of his race, and no discrimination against them because of color, has been asserted in a number of cases. So, where the laws of a particular locality or the charter of a particular railway corporation has provided that no person shall be excluded from the cars on account of color, we have held that this meant that persons of color should travel in the same car as white ones, and that the enactment was not satisfied by the company's providing cars assigned exclusively to people of color, though they were as good as those which they assigned exclusively to white persons. *Railroad Company v. Brown,* 17 Wall. 445.

Upon the other hand, where a statute of Louisiana required those engaged in the transportation of passengers among the States to give to all persons travelling within that State, upon vessels employed in that business, equal rights and privileges in all parts of the vessel, without distinction on account of race or color, and subject to an action for damages the owner of such a vessel, who excluded colored passengers on account of their color from the cabin set aside by him for the use of whites, it was held to be so far as it applied to interstate commerce, unconstitutional and void. *Hall v. De Cuir,* 95 U.S. 485. The court in this case, however, expressly disclaimed that it had anything whatever to do with the statute as a regulation of internal commerce, or affecting anything else than commerce among the States.

In the *Civil Rights Case,* 109 U.S. 3, it was held that an act of Congress, entitling all persons within the jurisdiction of the United States to the full and equal enjoyment of the accommodations, advantages, facilities and privileges of inns, public conveyances, on land or water, theatres and other places of public amusement, and made applicable to citizens of every race and color, regardless of any previous condition of servitude, was unconstitutional and void, upon the ground that the Fourteenth Amendment was prohibitory upon the States only, and the legislation authorized to be adopted by Congress for enforcing it was not direct legislation on matters respecting which the States were prohibited from making or enforcing certain laws, or doing certain acts, but was corrective legislation, such as might be necessary or proper for counteracting and redressing the effect of such laws or acts. In delivering the opinion of the court Mr. Justice Bradley observed that the Fourteenth Amendment "does not invest Congress with power to legislate upon subjects that are within the domain of state legislation; but to provide modes of relief against state legislation, or state action, of the kind referred to. It does not authorize Congress to create a code of municipal law for the regulation of private rights; but to provide modes of redress against the operation of state laws, and the action of state officers, executive or judicial, when these are subversive of the fundamental rights specified in the amendment. Positive rights and privileges are undoubtedly secured by the Fourteenth Amendment; but they are secured by way of prohibition against state laws and state proceedings affecting those rights and privileges, and by power given to Congress to legislate for the purpose of carrying such prohibition into effect; and such legislation must necessarily be predicated upon such supposed state laws or state proceedings, and be directed to the correction of their operation and effect."

Much nearer, and, indeed, almost directly in point, is the case of the *Louisville, New Orleans and Railway v. Mississippi,* 133 U. S. 587, wherein the railway company was indicted for a violation of a statute of Mississippi, enacting that all railroads carrying passengers should provide equal, but separate, accommodations for the white and colored races, by providing two or more passenger cars for each passenger train, or by dividing the passenger cars by a partition, so as to secure separate accommodations. The case was presented in a different aspect from the one under consideration, inasmuch as it was an indictment against the railway company for failing to provide the separate accommodations, but the question considered was the constitutionality of the law. In that case, the Supreme Court of Mississippi, 66 Mississippi, 662, had held that the statute applied solely to commerce within the State, and, that being the construction of the state statute by its highest court, was accepted as conclusive. "If it be a matter," said the court, p. 591, "respecting commerce wholly within a State, and not interfering with commerce between the States, then, obviously, there is no violation of the commerce clause of the Federal Constitution. . . . No question arises under this section, as to the power of the State to separate in different compartments interstate passengers, or affect, in any manner, the privileges and rights of such passengers. All that we can consider is, whether the State has the power to require that railroad trains within her limits shall have separate accommodations for the two races; that affecting only commerce within the State is no invasion of the power given to Congress by the commerce clause."

A like course of reasoning applies to the case under consideration, since the Supreme Court of Louisiana in the case of the *State ex rel. Abbott v. Hicks, Judge, et al.*, 44 La. Ann. 770, held that the statute in question did not apply to interstate passengers, but was confined in its application to passengers travelling exclusively within the borders of the State. The case was decided largely upon the authority of *Railway Co. v. State*, 66 Mississippi, 662, and affirmed by this court in 133 U.S. 587. In the present case no question of interference with interstate commerce can possibly arise, since the East Louisiana Railway appears to have been purely a local line, with both its termini within the State of Louisiana. Similar statutes for the separation of the two races upon public conveyances were held to be constitutional.

While we think the enforced separation of the races, as applied to the internal commerce of the State, neither abridges the privileges or immunities of the colored man, deprives him of his property without due process of law, nor denies him the equal protection of the laws, within the meaning of the Fourteenth Amendment, we are not prepared to say that the conductor, in assigning passengers to the coaches according to their race, does not act at his peril, or that the provision of the second section of the act, that denies to the passenger compensation in damages for a refusal to receive him into the coach in which he properly belongs, is a valid exercise of the legislative power. Indeed, we understand it to be conceded by the State's attorney, that such part of the act as exempts from liability the railway company and its officers is unconstitutional. The power to assign to a particular coach obviously implies the power to determine to which race the passenger belongs, as well as the power to determine who, under the laws of the particular State, is to be deemed a white, and who a colored person. This question, though indicated in the brief of the plaintiff in error, does not properly arise upon the unconstitutionality of the act, so far as it requires the railway to provide separate accommodations, and the conductor to assign passengers according to their race.

It is claimed by the plaintiff in error that, in any mixed community, the reputation of belonging to the dominant race, in this instance the white race, is *property*, in the same sense that a right of action, or of inheritance, is property. Conceding this to be so, for the purposes of this case, we are unable to see how this statute deprives him of, or in any way affects his right to, such property. If he be a white man and assigned to a colored coach, he may have his action for damages against the company for being deprived of his so called property. Upon the other hand, if he be a colored man and be so assigned, he has been deprived of no property, since he is not lawfully entitled to the reputation of being a white man.

In this connection, it is also suggested by the learned counsel for the plaintiff in error that the same argument that will justify the state legislature in requiring railways to provide separate accommodations for the two races will also authorize them to require separate cars to be provided for people whose hair is of a certain color, or who are aliens, or who belong to certain nationalities, or to enact laws requiring colored people to walk upon one side of the street, and white people upon the other, or requiring white men's houses to be painted white, and colored men's black, or their vehicles or business signs to be of different colors, upon the theory that one side of the street is as good as the other, or that a house or vehicle of one color is as good as one of another color. The reply to all this is that every exercise of the police power must be reasonable, and extend only to such laws as are enacted in good faith for the promotion of the public good, and not for the annoyance or oppression of a particular class. Thus in *Yick Wo v. Hopkins*, 118 U.S. 356, it was held by this court that a municipal ordinance of the city of San Francisco, to regulate the carrying on of public laundries within the limits of the municipality, violated the provisions of the Constitution of the United States, if it conferred upon the municipal authorities arbitrary power, at their own will, and without regard to discretion, in the legal sense of the term, to give or withhold consent as to persons or places, without regard to the competency of the persons applying, or the propriety of the places selected for the carrying on of the business. It was held to be a covert attempt on the part of the municipality to make an arbitrary and unjust discrimination against the Chinese race. While this was the case of a municipal ordinance, a like principle has been held to apply to acts of a state legislature passed in the exercise of the police power.

So far, then, as a conflict with the Fourteenth Amendment is concerned, the case reduces itself to the question whether the statute of Louisiana is a reasonable regulation, and with respect to this there must necessarily be a large discretion on the part of the legislature. In determining the question of reasonableness it is at liberty to act with reference to the established usages, customs and traditions of the people, and with a view to the promotion of their comfort, and the preservation of the public peace and good order. Gauged by this standard, we cannot say that a law which authorizes or even requires the separation of the two races in public conveyances is unreasonable, or more obnoxious to the Fourteenth Amendment than the acts of Congress requiring separate schools for colored children in the District of Columbia, the constitutionality of which does not seem to have been questioned, or the corresponding acts of state legislatures.

We consider the underlying fallacy of the plaintiff's argument to consist in the assumption that the enforced separation of the two races stamps the colored race with a badge of inferiority. If this be so, it is not by reason of anything found in the act, but solely because the colored race chooses to put that construction upon it. The argument necessarily assumes that if, as has been more than once the case, and is not unlikely to be so again, the colored race should become the dominant power in the state legislature, and should enact a law in precisely similar terms, it would thereby relegate the white race to an inferior position. We imagine that the white race, at least, would not acquiesce in this assumption. The argument also assumes that social prejudices may be overcome by legislation, and that equal rights cannot be secured to the negro except by an enforced commingling of the two races. We cannot accept this proposition. If the two races are to meet upon terms of social equality, it must be the result of natural affinities, a mutual appreciation of each other's merits and a voluntary consent of individuals. As was said by the Court of Appeals of New York in *People v. Gallagher,* 93 N.Y. 438, 448, "this end can neither be accomplished nor promoted by laws which conflict with the general sentiment of the community upon whom they are designed to operate. When the government, therefore, has secured to each of its citizens equal rights before the law and equal opportunities for improvement and progress, it has accomplished the end for which it was organized and performed all of the functions respecting social advantages with which it is endowed." Legislation is powerless to eradicate racial instincts or to abolish distinctions based upon physical differences, and the attempt to do so can only result in accentuating the difficulties of the present situation. If the civil and political rights of both races be equal one cannot be inferior to the other civilly or politically. If one race be inferior to the other socially, the Constitution of the United States cannot put them upon the same plane.

It is true that the question of the proportion of colored blood necessary to constitute a colored person, as distinguished from a white person, is one upon which there is a difference of opinion in the different States, some holding that any visible admixture of black blood stamps the person as belonging to the colored race; others that it depends upon the preponderance of blood; and still others that the predominance of white blood must only be in the proportion of three fourths. But these are questions to be determined under the laws of each State and are not properly put in issue in this case. Under the allegations of his petition it may undoubtedly become a question of importance whether, under the law of Louisiana, the petitioner belongs to the white or colored race.

The judgment of the court below is, therefore, *Affirmed.*

Mr. Justice Harlan dissenting.

By the Louisiana statute, the validity of which is here involved, all railway companies (other than street railroad companies) carrying passengers in that State are required to have separate but equal accommodations for white and colored persons, "by providing two or more passenger coaches for each passenger train, *or* by dividing the passenger coaches by a *partition* so as to secure separate accommodations." Under this statute, no colored person is permitted to occupy a seat in a coach assigned to white persons; nor any white person, to occupy a seat in a coach assigned to colored persons. The managers of the railroad are not allowed to exercise any discretion in the premises, but are required to assign each passenger to some coach or compartment set apart for the exclusive use of his race. If a passenger insists upon going into a coach or compartment not set apart for persons of his race, he is subject to be fined, or to be imprisoned in the parish jail. Penalties are prescribed for the refusal or neglect of the officers, directors, conductors and employés of railroad companies to comply with the provisions of the act.

Only "nurses attending children of the other race" are excepted from the operation of the statute. No exception is made of colored attendants travelling with adults. A white man is not permitted to have his colored servant with him in the same coach, even if his condition of health requires the constant, personal assistance of such servant. If a colored maid insists upon riding in the same coach with a white woman whom she has been employed to serve, and who may need her personal attention while travelling, she is subject to be fined or imprisoned for such an exhibition of zeal in the discharge of duty.

While there may be in Louisiana persons of different races who are not citizens of the United States, the words in the act, "white and colored races," necessarily include all citizens of the United States of both races residing in that State. So that we have before us a state enactment that compels, under penalties, the separation of the two races in railroad passenger coaches, and makes it a crime for a citizen of either race to enter a coach that has been assigned to citizens of the other race.

Thus the State regulates the use of a public highway by citizens of the United States solely upon the basis of race.

However apparent the injustice of such legislation may be, we have only to consider whether it is consistent with the Constitution of the United States.

That a railroad is a public highway, and that the corporation which owns or operates it is in the exercise of public functions, is not, at this day, to be disputed. Mr. Justice Nelson, speaking for this court in *New Jersey Steam Navigation Co. v. Merchants' Bank,* 6 How. 344, 382, said that a common carrier was in the exercise "of a sort of public office, and has public duties to perform, from which he should not be permitted to exonerate himself without the assent of the parties concerned." Mr. Justice Strong, delivering the judgment of the court in *Olcott v. The Supervisors,* 16 Wall. 678, 694, said: "That railroads, though constructed by private corporations and owned by them, are public highways, has been the doctrine of nearly all the courts ever since such conveniences for passage and transportation have had any existence. Very early the question arose whether a State's right of eminent domain could be exercised by a private corporation created for the purpose of constructing a railroad. Clearly it could not, unless taking land for such a purpose by such an agency is taking land for public use. The right of eminent domain nowhere justifies taking property for a private use. Yet it is a doctrine universally accepted that a state legislature may authorize a private corporation to take land for the construction of such a road, making compensation to the owner. What else does this doctrine mean if not that building a railroad, though it be built by a private corporation, is an act done for a public use?" So, in *Township of Pine Grove v. Talcott,* 19 Wall. 666, 676: "Though the corporation [a railroad company] was private, its work was public, as much so as if it were to be constructed by the State." So, in *Inhabitants of Worcester v. Western Railroad Corporation,* 4 Met. 564: "The establishment of that great thoroughfare is regarded as a public work, established by public authority, intended for the public use and benefit, the use of which is secured to the whole community, and constitutes, therefore, like a canal, turnpike or highway, a public easement." It is true that the real and personal property, necessary to the establishment and management of the railroad, is vested in the corporation; but it is in trust for the public."

In respect to civil rights, common to all citizens, the Constitution of the United States does not, I think, permit any public authority to know the race of those entitled to be protected in the enjoyment of such rights. Every true man has pride of race, and under appropriate circumstances when the rights of others, his equals before the law, are not to be affected, it is his privilege to express such pride and to take such action based upon it as to him seems proper. But I deny that any legislative body or judicial tribunal may have regard to the race of citizens when the civil rights of those citizens are involved. Indeed, such legislation, as that here in question, is inconsistent not only with that equality of rights which pertains to citizenship, National and State, but with the personal liberty enjoyed by every one within the United States.

The Thirteenth Amendment does not permit the withholding or the deprivation of any right necessarily inhering in freedom. It not only struck down the institution of slavery as previously existing in the United States, but it prevents the imposition of any burdens or disabilities that constitute badges of slavery or servitude. It decreed universal civil freedom in this country. This court has so adjudged. But that amendment having been found inadequate to the protection of the rights of those who had been in slavery, it was followed by the Fourteenth Amendment, which added greatly to the dignity and glory of American citizenship, and to the security of personal liberty, by declaring that "all persons born or naturalized in the United States, and subject to the jurisdiction thereof, are citizens of the United States and of the State wherein they reside," and that "no State shall make or enforce any law which shall abridge the privileges or immunities of citizens of the United States; nor shall any State deprive any person of life, liberty or property without due process of law, nor deny to any person within its jurisdiction the equal protection of the laws." These two amendments, if enforced according to their true intent and meaning, will protect all the civil rights that pertain to freedom and citizenship. Finally, and to the end that no citizen should be denied, on account of his race, the privilege of participating in the political control of his country, it was declared by the Fifteenth Amendment that "the right of citizens of the United States to vote shall not be denied or abridged by the United States or by any State on account of race, color or previous condition of servitude."

These notable additions to the fundamental law were welcomed by the friends of liberty throughout the world. They removed the race line from our governmental systems. They had, as this court has said, a common purpose, namely, to secure "to a race recently emancipated, a race that through many generations have been held in slavery, all the civil rights that the superior race enjoy." They declared, in legal effect, this court has further said, "that the law in the States shall be the same for the black as for the white; that all persons, whether colored or white, shall stand equal before the laws of the States, and, in regard to the colored race, for whose protection the amendment was primarily designed, that no discrimination shall be made against them by law because of their color." We also said: "The words of the amendment, it is true, are prohibitory, but they contain a necessary implication of a positive immunity, or right, most valuable to the colored race – the right to exemption from unfriendly legislation against them distinctively as colored – exemption from legal discriminations, implying inferiority in civil society, lessening the security of their enjoyment of the rights which others enjoy, and discriminations which are steps towards reducing them to the condition of a subject race." It was, consequently, adjudged that a state law that excluded citizens of the colored race from juries, because of their race and however well qualified in other respects to discharge the duties of jurymen, was repugnant to the Fourteenth Amendment. At the present term, referring to the previous adjudications, this court declared that "underlying all of those decisions is the principle that the Constitution of the United States, in its present form, forbids, so far as civil and political rights are concerned, discrimination by the General Government or the States against any citizen because of his race. All citizens are equal before the law."

The decisions referred to show the scope of the recent amendments of the Constitution. They also show that it is not within the power of a State to prohibit colored citizens, because of their race, from participating as jurors in the administration of justice.

It was said in argument that the statute of Louisiana does not discriminate against either race, but prescribes a rule applicable alike to white and colored citizens. But this argument does not meet the difficulty. Every one knows that the statute in question had its origin in the purpose, not so much to exclude white persons from railroad cars occupied by blacks, as to exclude colored people from coaches occupied by or assigned to white persons. Railroad corporations of Louisiana did not make discrimination among whites in the matter of accommodation for travellers. The thing to accomplish was, under the guise of giving equal accommodation for whites and blacks, to compel the latter to keep to themselves while travelling in railroad passenger coaches. No one would be so wanting in candor as to assert the contrary. The fundamental objection, therefore, to the statute is that it interferes with the personal freedom of citizens. "Personal liberty," it has been well said, "consists in the power of locomotion, of changing situation, or removing one's person to whatsoever places one's own inclination may direct, without imprisonment or restraint, unless by due course of law." If a white man and a black man choose to occupy the same public conveyance on a public highway, it is their right to do so, and no government, proceeding alone on grounds of race, can prevent it without infringing the personal liberty of each.

It is one thing for railroad carriers to furnish, or to be required by law to furnish, equal accommodations for all whom they are under a legal duty to carry. It is quite another thing for government to forbid citizens of the white and black races from travelling in the same public conveyance, and to punish officers of railroad companies for permitting persons of the two races to occupy the same passenger coach. If a State can prescribe, as a rule of civil conduct, that whites and blacks shall not travel as passengers in the same railroad coach, why may it not so regulate the use of the streets of its cities and towns as to compel white citizens to keep on one side of a street and black citizens to keep on the other? Why may it not, upon like grounds, punish whites and blacks who ride together in street cars or in open vehicles on a public road or street? Why may it not require sheriffs to assign whites to one side of a court-room and blacks to the other? And why may it not also prohibit the commingling of the two races in the galleries of legislative halls or in public assemblages convened for the consideration of the political questions of the day? Further, if this statute of Louisiana is consistent with the personal liberty of citizens, why may not the State require the separation in railroad coaches of native and naturalized citizens of the United States, or of Protestants and Roman Catholics?

The answer given at the argument to these questions was that regulations of the kind they suggest would be unreasonable, and could not, therefore, stand before the law. Is it meant that the determination of questions of legislative power depends upon the inquiry whether the statute whose validity is questioned is, in the judgment of the courts, a reasonable one, taking all the circumstances into consideration? A statute may be unreasonable merely because a sound public policy forbade its enactment. But I do not understand that the courts have anything to do with the policy or expediency of legislation. A statute may be valid, and yet, upon grounds of public policy, may well be characterized as unreasonable. Mr. Sedgwick correctly states the rule when he says that the legislative intention being clearly ascertained, "the courts have no other duty to perform than to execute the legislative will, without any regard to their views as to the wisdom or justice of the particular enactment." There is a dangerous tendency in these latter days to enlarge the functions of the courts, by means of judicial interference with the will of the people as expressed by the legislature. Our institutions have the distinguishing characteristic that the three departments of government are coördinate and separate. Each must keep within the limits defined by the Constitution. And the courts best discharge their duty by executing the will of the law-making power, constitutionally expressed, leaving the results of legislation to be dealt with by the people through their representatives. Statutes might always have a reasonable construction. Sometimes they are to be construed strictly; sometimes, liberally, in order to carry out the legislative will. But however construed, the intent of the legislature is to be respected, if the particular statute in question is valid, although the courts, looking at the public interests, may conceive the statute to be both unreasonable and impolitic. If the power exists to enact a statute, that ends the matter so far as the courts are concerned. The adjudged cases in which statutes have been held to be void, because unreasonable, are those in which the means employed by the legislature were not at all germane to the end to which the legislature was competent.

The white race deems itself to be the dominant race in this country. And so it is, in prestige, in achievements, in education, in wealth and in power. So, I doubt not, it will continue to be for all time, if it remains true to its great heritage and holds fast to the principles of constitutional liberty. But in view of the Constitution, in the eye of the law, there is in this country no superior, dominant, ruling class of citizens. There is no caste here. Our Constitution is color-blind, and neither knows nor tolerates classes among citizens. In respect of civil rights, all citizens are equal before the law. The humblest is the peer of the most powerful. The law regards man as man, and takes no account of his surroundings or of his color when his civil rights as guaranteed by the supreme law of the land are involved. It is, therefore, to be regretted that this high tribunal, the final expositor of the fundamental law of the land, has reached the conclusion that it is competent for a State to regulate the enjoyment by citizens of their civil rights solely upon the basis of race.

In my opinion, the judgment this day rendered will, in time, prove to be quite as pernicious as the decision made by this tribunal in the *Dred Scott case.* It was adjudged in that case that the descendants of Africans who were imported into this country and sold as slaves were not included nor intended to be included under the word "citizens" in the Constitution, and could not claim any of the rights and privileges which that instrument provided for and secured to citizens of the United States; that at the time of the adoption of the Constitution they were "considered as a subordinate and inferior class of beings, who had been subjugated by the dominant race, and, whether emancipated or not, yet remained subject to their authority, and had no rights or privileges but such as those who held the power and the government might choose to grant them." The recent amendments of the Constitution, it was supposed, had eradicated these principles from our institutions. But it seems that we have yet, in some of the States, a dominant race – a superior class of citizens, which assumes to regulate the enjoyment of civil rights, common to all citizens, upon the basis of race. The present decision, it may well be apprehended, will not only stimulate aggressions, more or less brutal and irritating, upon the admitted rights of colored citizens, but will encourage the belief that it is possible, by means of state enactments, to defeat the beneficent purposes which the people of the United States had in view when they adopted the recent amendments of the Constitution, by one of which the blacks of this country were made citizens of the United States and of the States in which they respectively reside, and whose privileges and immunities, as citizens, the States are forbidden to abridge. Sixty millions of whites are in no danger from the presence here of eight millions of blacks. The destinies of the two races, in this country, are indissolubly linked together, and the interests of both require that the common government of all shall not permit the seeds of race hate to be planted under the sanction of law. What can more certainly arouse race hate, what more certainly create and perpetuate a feeling of distrust between these races, than state enactments, which, in fact, proceed on the ground that colored citizens are so inferior and degraded that they cannot be allowed to sit in public coaches occupied by white citizens? That, as all will admit, is the real meaning of such legislation as was enacted in Louisiana.

The sure guarantee of the peace and security of each race is the clear, distinct, unconditional recognition by our governments, National and State, of every right that inheres in civil freedom, and of the equality before the law of all citizens of the United States without regard to race. State enactments, regulating the enjoyment of civil rights, upon the basis of race, and cunningly devised to defeat legitimate results of the war, under the pretence of recognizing equality of rights, can have no other result than to render permanent peace impossible, and to keep alive a conflict of races, the continuance of which must do harm to all concerned. This question is not met by the suggestion that social equality cannot exist between the white and black races in this country. That argument, if it can be properly regarded as one, is scarcely worthy of consideration; for social equality no more exists between two races when travelling in a passenger coach or on a public highway than when members of the same races sit by each other in a street car or in the jury box, or stand or sit with each other in a political assembly, or when they use in common the streets of a city or town, or when they are in the same room for the purpose of having their names placed on the registry of voters, or when they approach the ballot-box in order to exercise the high privilege of voting.

There is a race so different from our own that we do not permit those belonging to it to become citizens of the United States. Persons belonging to it are, with few exceptions, absolutely excluded from our country. I allude to the Chinese race. But by the statute in question, a Chinaman can ride in the same passenger coach with white citizens of the United States, while citizens of the black race in Louisiana, many of whom, perhaps, risked their lives for the preservation of the Union, who are entitled, by law, to participate in the political control of the State and nation, who are not excluded, by law or by reason of their race, from public stations of any kind, and who have all the legal rights that belong to white citizens, are yet declared to be criminals, liable to imprisonment, if they ride in a public coach occupied by citizens of the white race. It is scarcely just to say that a colored citizen should not object to occupying a public coach assigned to his own race. He does not object, nor, perhaps, would he object to separate coaches for his race, if his rights under the law were recognized. But he objects, and ought never to cease objecting to the proposition, that citizens of the white and black races can be adjudged criminals because they sit, or claim the right to sit, in the same public coach on a public highway.

The arbitrary separation of citizens, on the basis of race, while they are on a public highway, is a badge of servitude wholly inconsistent with the civil freedom and the equality before the law established by the Constitution. It cannot be justified upon any legal grounds.

If evils will result from the commingling of the two races upon public highways established for the benefit of all, they will be infinitely less than those that will surely come from state legislation regulating the enjoyment of civil rights upon the basis of race. We boast of the freedom enjoyed by our people above all other peoples. But it is difficult to reconcile that boast with a state of the law which, practically, puts the brand of servitude and degradation upon a large class of our fellow-citizens, our equals before the law. The thin disguise of "equal" accommodations for passengers in railroad coaches will not mislead any one, nor atone for the wrong this day done.

The result of the whole matter is, that while this court has frequently adjudged, and at the present term has recognized the doctrine, that a State cannot, consistently with the Constitution of the United States, prevent white and black citizens, having the required qualifications for jury service, from sitting in the same jury box, it is now solemnly held that a State may prohibit white and black citizens from sitting in the same passenger coach on a public highway, or may require that they be separated by a "partition," when in the same passenger coach. May it not now be reasonably expected that astute men of the dominant race, who affect to be disturbed at the possibility that the integrity of the white race may be corrupted, or that its supremacy will be imperilled, by contact on public highways with black people, will endeavor to procure statutes requiring white and black jurors to be separated in the jury box by a "partition," and that, upon retiring from the court room to consult as to their verdict, such partition, if it be a moveable one, shall be taken to their consultation room, and set up in such way as to prevent black jurors from coming too close to their brother jurors of the white race. If the "partition" used in the court room happens to be stationary, provision could be made for screens with openings through which jurors of the two races could confer as to their verdict without coming into personal contact with each other. I cannot see but that, according to the principles this day announced, such state legislation, although conceived in hostility to, and enacted for the purpose of humiliating citizens of the United States of a particular race, would be held to be consistent with the Constitution.

I do not deem it necessary to review the decisions of state courts to which reference was made in argument. Some, and the most important, of them are wholly inapplicable, because rendered prior to the adoption of the last amendments of the Constitution, when colored people had very few rights which the dominant race felt obliged to respect. Others were made at a time when public opinion, in many localities, was dominated by the institution of slavery; when it would not have been safe to do justice to the black man; and when, so far as the rights of blacks were concerned, race prejudice was, practically, the supreme law of the land. Those decisions cannot be guides in the era introduced by the recent amendments of the supreme law, which established universal civil freedom, gave citizenship to all born or naturalized in the United States and residing here, obliterated the race line from our systems of governments, National and State, and placed our free institutions upon the broad and sure foundation of the equality of all men before the law.

I am of opinion that the statute of Louisiana is inconsistent with the personal liberty of citizens, white and black, in that State, and hostile to both the spirit and letter of the Constitution of the United States. If laws of like character should be enacted in the several States of the Union, the effect would be in the highest degree mischievous. Slavery, as an institution tolerated by law would, it is true, have disappeared from our country, but there would remain a power in the States, by sinister legislation, to interfere with the full enjoyment of the blessings of freedom; to regulate civil rights, common to all citizens, upon the basis of race; and to place in a condition of legal inferiority a large body of American citizens, now constituting a part of the political community called the People of the United States, for whom, and by whom through representatives, our government is administered. Such a system is inconsistent with the guarantee given by the Constitution to each State of a republican form of government, and may be stricken down by Congressional action, or by the courts in the discharge of their solemn duty to maintain the supreme law of the land, anything in the constitution or laws of any State to the contrary notwithstanding.

For the reasons stated, I am constrained to withhold my assent from the opinion and judgment of the majority.

Robert A. Leflar and *Wylie H. Davis*:

THE SUPREME COURT CASES

THE Supreme Court's previous views on racial segregation in state-supported schools are fairly well-known to non-lawyers today. They originated with *Plessy v. Ferguson*, which in 1896 sustained a Louisiana statute requiring separate railroad accommodations for Negroes and whites and referred to the accepted practice of public school segregation as supporting that conclusion. This dictum stood practically by itself, save for lower federal and state court cases, until 1927 – when *Gong Lum v. Rice*[1] held that a child of Chinese ancestry could be required to attend schools established for the colored race in Mississippi without being thereby denied the equal protection of the laws guaranteed by the Fourteenth Amendment. The Court assumed "facilities for education equal to that offered to all" and said, "we think that it is the same question which has been many times decided to be within the constitutional power of the state legislature to settle without intervention of the federal courts under the Federal Constitution." Eleven years later, in the *Gaines*[2] case, the Court held that the Equal Protection Clause gave to the plaintiff Negro a personal right to require the State of Missouri "to furnish him within its borders facilities for legal education substantially equal to those which the State there afforded for persons of the white race." This made it clear that payment of tuition and expenses at out-of-state schools did not satisfy the constitutional requirement, but the decision was interpreted to permit a separate law school for Negroes in Missouri. The order in the *Sipuel*[3] cases, after another nine years had passed, was essentially the same, with only the difference in result that Oklahoma complied not by perse-

[1] *Gong Lum v. Rice*, 275 U.S. 78 (1927)

[2] *Missouri ex rel. Gaines v. Canada*, 305 U.S. 337 (1938)

[3] *Sipuel v. Board of Regents*, 332 U.S. 631 (1948)

From the *Harvard Law Review*, Vol. 67, January, 1954, No. 3, pp. 377–429. Reprinted by permission.

vering with a separate law school for Negroes but by admitting the applicant to the already existent school of the University of Oklahoma. Two years later in *Sweatt v. Painter*[4] the Court held that a makeshift separate law school for Negroes set up by the State of Texas did not afford "substantial equality" in legal educational opportunities for a colored plaintiff as compared with facilities available to white students at the University of Texas Law School, so that "the equal protection of the laws" entitled him to be admitted to the law school at the University. And in the *McLaurin*[5] case, decided at the same time, the holding was that the plaintiff Negro, a graduate student in education already admitted to the University of Oklahoma, was being denied equal educational opportunities by a specially devised system of intramural segregation which kept him apart from his fellow students while he was in the same rooms and classes with them. Even in this last case the Court's opinion was so framed as to base its conclusion on the fact of inequality of opportunity under the total circumstances rather than upon segregation alone. The Court did not say that segregation was inequality or that by itself it was a denial of the equal protection of the laws; it was able to render its decision without arriving at that issue.

Common understanding is that the five cases now pending before the Court do present squarely the issue whether segregation in public schools constitutes state action denying to Negroes the equal protection of the laws. . . .

Without guessing what position the Court will ultimately take in deciding the pending cases, it is possible to list most of the positions which it might take, and perhaps all of them. Some of those suggested are highly improbable and deserve inclusion only because they come within the historical framework of the race problem in America or because they represent points of view that may influence the Court, even negatively. . . .

1. If procedurally possible, the Court might avoid passing on the segregation issue at all. This would depend on the availability of less delicate grounds upon which each of the cases could be decided, under the rule that the Court will not anticipate a question of constitutional law in advance of the necessity of deciding it.

2. The "separate but equal" doctrine is still the law, and the Court will accept lower court fact-findings of "substantial equality" such as were characteristic of the older state cases, which really meant only nominal equality. Some of the lower federal courts, however, and a few state tribunals too, following the lead of *Gaines, Sipuel, Sweatt,* and *McLaurin,* have already held that under the "separate but equal" concept real equality is now required.

3. The "separate but equal" doctrine is still the law, and when the separate facilities are unequal the Court will allow additional time for bringing them to a state of substantial equality (which means real equality), under the direction of the lower courts.

4. The "separate but equal" doctrine is still the law, but when separate facilities are unequal the Court will require immediate admission of Negroes to the white schools pending achievement of actual equality in the Negro facilities.

5. Recognizing that the constitutionality of a particular state activity involving sociological relationships like segregated public schools may change with the

[4] *Sweatt v. Painter,* 339 U.S. 629 (1950)

[5] *McLaurin v. Oklahoma State Regents,* 339 U.S. 637 (1950)

times, and that the once valid "separate but equal" doctrine is diminishing in validity, the Court may yet conclude that it is not ready to condemn the doctrine as presently invalid but will undertake to wait a while longer before doing so. Although the Court would not of course state such a position in so many words, it might practically do the same thing by promulgating a compromise dressed up in nicely chosen legalisms.

6. The "separate but equal" doctrine is still the law, but in special situations segregation is inconsistent with equality. The practice might be allowable only in some but not all phases of the educational process. Thus it might be held that segregation in the major scholastic work of the classroom produces unconstitutional inequality, whereas it remains permissible in extra-curricular activities not materially affecting academic advancement. The opposite conclusion might also stem from the idea that psychological harm to young minds would accrue more from discrimination in extracurricular programs than from classroom segregation. Or it might be held that the validity of segregation depends on the field or type of education involved, full association with one's fellows being of great importance in some fields and less important in others.

7. Whether segregation in a given case amounts to unconstitutional inequality is a question of fact, to be decided like other questions of fact in the trial court. This would permit different results from case to case, the variances possible being influenced by whatever local social or emotional factors operate upon fact finders, whether judges or jurors, to produce divergent findings from substantially similar evidence.

8. The "separate but equal" doctrine is no longer valid and the Equal Protection Clause forbids public school segregation, but the Court will not itself undertake elaborate implementation; rather it will limit itself to minimum personal relief to the parties before it, leaving to Congress the duty of enacting general remedial legislation which will prescribe detailed rules for the future. The Court habitually regards some questions as primarily "political" in nature, by reason of their complex social and economic as well as emotional ramifications, particularly if decision calls for new rules to govern the future conduct of large numbers of persons in a new area of regulation. The legislative branch is better qualified to handle such questions than is the judicial, and so the Court remits them to the Congress.[6]

9. The "separate but equal" doctrine is no longer valid and the Equal Protection Clause forbids public school segregation, but a gradual correction of the unlawful situation extending over a period of time will be permitted, the Supreme Court giving general directions only as to the broad plan and the time within which a changeover is to be made, leaving the formulation of detailed orders and the supervision thereof to the lower courts.

10. Same as 9, above, except that with the aid of a master the Court itself would

[6] [As for this the authors say, "A realistic possibility, of course, is that Congress might, either by majority vote or in consequence of filibusters or other dilatory legislative devices, do little or nothing, thus practically disregarding any Supreme Court intimation that it should act in the matter. Certainly recent congressional history does not portend a quick enactment of comprehensive anti-discrimination laws in any field. Perhaps laws aimed at equalization rather than desegregation would fare better, although groups favoring elimination of segregation might oppose them for reasons of political and psychological policy. Remitting the matter to Congress without affirmative action under the Court's own constitutional power might well mean an indefinite postponement of effective action toward ending racial discrimination in the public schools." Ed.]

issue detailed orders, either retaining jurisdiction in the cases during the time fixed for compliance and presumably exercising its supervisory power through the appointed master, or returning the cases to the lower courts for continuing supervision of the compliance details.

11. The "separate but equal" doctrine is no longer valid and the Equal Protection Clause forbids public school segregation, which must end at once. In all cases before the Court, Negroes must be admitted to white schools, or the school systems in some other way racially integrated, forthwith, and state or local laws providing for separate schools are no longer to be enforced. Regardless of what the Court's decision may be, it will almost surely seem to the layman more far-reaching than it really is, since the ensuing orders will be directly applicable only in the cases and to the parties actually before the Court. Unless criminal proceedings be initiated, even United States marshals will not move in to enforce the Court's rulings. Voluntary compliance may be anticipated in some, perhaps in many, districts. In other districts, new litigation will have to be brought if compliance with pronouncements that go at all beyond the limits of present practices is to be achieved. In some sections of the country political and social pressures will probably forestall lawsuits for years to come, just as these pressures have done in most districts of the South in years gone by despite a general realization that the legal rights of Negroes even under the "separate but equal" doctrine were being denied.

From the BRIEFS SUBMITTED TO THE SUPREME COURT

THE four school segregation cases were argued and submitted to the Supreme Court on December 9–11, 1952. Thereafter, on June 8, 1953, the Supreme Court entered its order for reargument, as follows:

Each of these cases is ordered restored to the docket and is assigned for reargument on Monday, October 12, next. In their briefs and on oral argument counsel are requested to discuss particularly the following questions insofar as they are relevant to the respective cases:

1. What evidence is there that the Congress which submitted and the State legislatures and conventions which ratified the Fourteenth Amendment contemplated or did not contemplate, understood or did not understand, that it would abolish segregation in public schools?

2. If neither the Congress in submitting nor the States in ratifying the Fourteenth Amendment understood that compliance with it would require the immediate abolition of segregation in public schools, was it nevertheless the understanding of the framers of the Amendment

(a) that future Congresses might, in the exercise of their power under Sec. 5 of the Amendment, abolish such segregation, or

(b) that it would be within the judicial power, in light of future conditions, to construe the Amendment as abolishing such segregation of its own force?

3. On the assumption that the answers to questions 2(a) and (b) do not dispose of the issue, is it within the judicial power, in construing the Amendment, to abolish segregation in public schools?

4. Assuming it is decided that segregation in public schools violates the Fourteenth Amendment

(a) would a decree necessarily follow providing that, within the limits set by normal geographic school districting, Negro children should forthwith be admitted to schools of their choice, or

(b) may this Court, in the exercise of its equity powers, permit an effective gradual adjustment to be brought about from existing segregated systems to a system not based on color distinctions?

5. On the assumption on which questions 4(a) and (b) are based, and assuming further that this Court will exercise its equity powers to the end described in question 4(b),

(a) should this Court formulate detailed decrees in these cases;

(b) if so what specific issues should the decrees reach;

(c) should this Court appoint a special master to hear evidence with a view to recommending specific terms for such decrees;

(d) should this Court remand to the courts of first instance with directions to frame decrees in these cases, and if so, what general directions should the decrees of this Court include and what procedures should the courts of first instance follow in arriving at the specific terms of more detailed decrees?

The Attorney General of the United States is invited to take part in the oral argument and to file an additional brief if he so desires.

On August 4, 1953, upon motion of the Attorney General of the United States and without objection by the parties, the Supreme Court entered its order postponing the date assigned for reargument of these cases until December 7, 1953.

Summary of Argument for Negro Children (Appellants)

These cases consolidated for argument before this Court present in different factual contexts essentially the same ultimate legal questions.

The substantive question common to all is whether a state can, consistently with the Constitution, exclude children, solely on the ground that they are Negroes, from public schools which otherwise they would be qualified to attend. It is the thesis of this brief, submitted on behalf of the excluded children, that the answer to the question is in the negative: the Fourteenth Amendment prevents states from according differential treatment to American children on the basis of their color or race. Both the legal precedents and the judicial theories, discussed in Part I hereof, and the evidence concerning the intent of the framers of the Fourteenth Amendment and the understanding of the Congress and the ratifying states, developed in Part II hereof, support this proposition.

Denying this thesis, the school authorities, relying in part on language originating in this Court's opinion in *Plessy v. Ferguson*, 163 U. S. 537, urge that exclusion of Negroes, *qua* Negroes, from designated public schools is permissible when the excluded children are afforded admittance to other schools especially reserved for Negroes, *qua* Negroes, if such schools are equal.

The procedural question common to all the cases is the role to be played, and the time-table to be followed, by this Court and the lower courts in directing an end to the challenged exclusion, in the event that this Court determines, with respect to the substantive question, that exclusion of Negroes, *qua* Negroes, from public schools contravenes the Constitution.

The importance to our American democracy of the substantive question can hardly be overstated. The question is whether a nation founded on the proposition that "all men are created equal" is honoring its commitments to grant "due process of law" and "the equal protection of the laws" to all within its borders when it, or one of its constituent states, confers or denies benefits on the basis of color or race.

1. Distinctions drawn by state authorities on the basis of color or race violate the Fourteenth Amendment. *Shelley v. Kraemer*, 334 U. S. 1; *Buchanan v. Warley*, 245 U. S. 60. This has been held to be true even as to the conduct of public educational institutions. *Sweatt v. Painter*, 339 U. S. 629; *McLaurin v. Oklahoma State Regents*, 339 U. S. 637. Whatever other purposes the Fourteenth Amendment may have had, it is indisputable that its primary purpose was to complete the emancipation provided by the Thirteenth Amendment by ensuring to the Negro equality before the law. The *Slaughter House Cases,* 16 Wall. 36; *Strauder v. West Virginia,* 100 U. S. 303.

2. Even if the Fourteenth Amendment did not *per se* invalidate racial distinctions as a matter of law, the racial segregation challenged in the instant cases would run afoul of the conventional test established for application of the equal protection clause because the racial classifications here have no reasonable relation to any valid legislative purpose. See *Quaker City Cab Co. v. Pennsylvania,* 277 U. S. 389; *Truax v. Raich,* 239 U. S. 33; *Smith v. Cahoon,* 283 U. S. 553; *Mayflower Farms v. Ten Eyck,* 297 U. S. 266; *Skinner v. Oklahoma,* 316 U. S. 535. See also *Tunstall v. Brotherhood of Locomotive Firemen,* 323 U. S. 210; *Steele v. Louisville & Nashville R. R. Co.*, 323 U. S. 192.

3. Appraisal of the facts requires rejection of the contention of the school authorities. The educational detriment involved in racially constricting a student's associations has already been recognized by this Court. *Sweatt v. Painter,* 339 U. S. 629; *McLaurin v. Oklahoma State Regents*, 339 U. S. 637.

4. The argument that the requirements of the Fourteenth Amendment are met by providing alternative schools rests, finally, on reiteration of the separate but equal doctrine enunciated in *Plessy v. Ferguson.*

Were these ordinary cases, it might be enough to say that the *Plessy* case can be distinguished – that it involved only segregation in transportation. But these are not ordinary cases, and in deference to their importance it seems more fitting to meet the *Plessy* doctrine head-on and to declare that doctrine erroneous.

Candor requires recognition that the plain purpose and effect of segregated education is to perpetuate an inferior status for Negroes which is America's sorry heritage from slavery. But the primary purpose of the Fourteenth Amendment was to deprive the states of *all* power to perpetuate such a caste system.

5. The first and second of the five questions propounded by this Court requested enlightment (sic) as to whether the Congress which submitted, and the state legislatures and conventions which ratified, the Fourteenth Amendment contemplated or understood that it would prohibit segregation in public schools, either of its own force or through subsequent legislative or judicial action. The evidence, both in Congress and in the legislatures of the ratifying states, reflects the substantial intent of the Amendment's proponents and the substantial understanding of its opponents that the Fourteenth Amendment would, of its own force, proscribe all forms of state-imposed racial distinctions, thus necessarily including all racial segregation in public education.

The Fourteenth Amendment was actually the culmination of the determined efforts of the Radical Republican majority in Congress to incorporate into our fundamental law the well-defined equalitarian principle of complete equality for all without regard to race or color. The debates in the 39th Congress and succeeding Congresses clearly reveal the intention that the Fourteenth Amendment would work a revolutionary change in our state-federal relationship by denying to the states the power to distinguish on the basis of race.

The Civil Rights Bill of 1866, as originally proposed, possessed scope sufficiently broad in the opinion of many Congressmen to entirely destroy all state legislation based on race. A great majority of the Republican Radicals – who later formulated the Fourteenth Amendment – understood and intended that the Bill would prohibit segregated schools. Opponents of the measure shared this understanding. The scope of this legislation was narrowed because it was known that the Fourteenth Amendment was in process of preparation and would itself have scope exceeding that of the original draft of the Civil Rights Bill.

6. The evidence makes clear that it was the intent of the proponents of the Fourteenth Amendment, and the substantial understanding of its opponents, that it would, of its own force, prohibit all state action predicated upon race or color. The intention of the framers with respect to any specific example of caste state action – in the instant cases, segregated education – cannot be determined solely on the basis of a tabulation of contemporaneous statements mentioning the specific practice. The framers were formulating a constitutional provision setting broad standards for determination of the relationship of the state to the individual. In the nature of things they could not list all the specific categories of existing and prospective state activity which were to come within the constitutional prohibitions. The broad general purpose of the Amendment – obliteration of race and color distinctions – is clearly established by the evidence. So far as there was consideration of the Amendment's impact upon the undeveloped educational systems then existing, both proponents and opponents of the Amendment understood that it would proscribe all racial segregation in public education.

7. While the Amendment conferred upon Congress the power to enforce its prohibitions, members of the 39th Congress and those of subsequent Congresses made it clear that the framers understood and intended that the Fourteenth Amendment was self-executing and particularly pointed out that the federal judiciary had authority to enforce its prohibitions without Congressional implementation.

8. The evidence as to the understanding of the states is equally convincing. Each of the eleven states that had seceded from the Union ratified the Amendment, and concurrently eliminated racial distinctions from its laws, and adopted a constitution free of requirement or specific authorization of segregated schools. Many rejected proposals for segregated schools, and none enacted a school segregation law until after readmission. The significance of these facts is manifest from the consideration that ten of these states, which were required, as a condition of readmission, to ratify the Amendment and to modify their constitutions and laws in conformity therewith, considered that the Amendment required them to remove all racial distinctions from their existing and prospective laws, including those pertaining to public education.

Twenty-two of the twenty-six Union states also ratified the Amendment. Although unfettered by congressional surveillance, the overwhelming majority of the Union states acted with an understanding that it prohibited racially segregated schools and necessitated conformity of their school laws to secure consistency with that understanding.

9. In short, the historical evidence fully sustains this Court's conclusion in the *Slaughter Houses Cases,* 16 Wall. 36, 81, that the Fourteenth Amendment was designed to take from the states all power to enforce caste or class distinctions.

10. The Court in its fourth and fifth questions assumes that segregation is declared unconstitutional and inquires as to whether relief should be granted immediately or gradually. Appellants, recognizing the possibility of delay of a purely administrative character, do not ask for the impossible. No cogent reasons justifying further exercise of equitable discretion, however, have as yet been produced.

It has been indirectly suggested in the briefs and oral argument of appellees that some such reasons exist. Two plans were suggested by the United States in its Brief as *Amicus Curiae.* We have analyzed each of these plans as well as appellees' briefs and oral argument and find nothing there of sufficient merit on which this Court, in the exercise of its equity power, could predicate a decree permitting an effective gradual adjustment from segregated to non-segregated school systems. Nor have we been able to find any other reasons or plans sufficient to warrant the exercise of such equitable discretion in these cases. Therefore, in the present posture of these cases, appellants are unable to suggest any compelling reasons for this Court to postpone relief.

Summary of Argument for School Boards (Appellees)

Answering the First Question: The overwhelming preponderance of the evidence demonstrates that the Congress which submitted and the State legislatures which ratified the Fourteenth Amendment did not contemplate and did not understand that it would abolish segregation in public schools.

There were 37 States in the Union at the time of the ratification of the Amendment. There is affirmative evidence from 23 of these States that it was understood that the Amendment would not abolish school segregation. In 14 States, no evidence, either affirmative or negative, is available. In not one State have we found substantial affirmative evidence that it was either contemplated or understood that ratification of the Amendment would mean that segregation in the public schools was abolished.

Answering the Second Question: It was not the understanding of the framers of the Amendment that future Congresses might, in the exercise of their power under Section 5 of the Amendment, abolish segregation in public schools; nor was it the understanding of the framers of the Amendment that it would be within the judicial power, in light of future conditions, to construe the Amendment as abolishing segregation in public schools of its own force.

Answering the Third Question: It is not within the judicial power to construe the Fourteenth Amendment adversely to the understanding of its framers, as abolishing segregation in the public schools. Moreover, if, in construing the Amendment, the principle of stare decisis is applied, controlling precedents preclude a construction which would abolish or forbid segregation in the public schools. Even if the principle of stare decisis and the controlling precedents be abandoned, and the effect of the Amendment upon public school segregation be examined *de novo,* under established standards of equal protection the Amendment may not be construed to abolish or forbid segregation as a matter of law and *a priori* in all cases. Rather, each case of such segregation must be decided upon the facts presented in the record of that case; and unless the record establishes by clear and convincing evidence that school segregation could not conceivably be warranted by local conditions in the particular case, the Fourteenth Amendment may not be construed to abolish segregation in that case.

Answering the Fourth Question: Assuming that it is decided – improperly, as we contend – that segregation in public schools violates the Fourteenth Amendment, a decree would not necessarily follow providing that, within the limits set by normal geographical school districting, Negro children should forthwith be admitted to schools of their own choice. This Court, in the exercise of its equity powers, may permit an effective gradual adjustment to be brought about from existing segregated systems to a system not based on color distinctions.

Answering the Fifth Question: Again assuming it is decided – improperly, as we contend – that segregation in public schools violates the Fourteenth Amendment, this Court should not, and indeed could not, formulate a detailed decree in this case; nor should this Court appoint a special master to hear evidence with a view to recommending specific terms for such a decree. Rather, this Court should remand the question to the District Court for further proceedings in conformity with this Court's opinion.

The answers to these questions in appellants' brief rest on certain fundamental fallacies. These are:

First, the fallacy that the antislavery crusade was directed against segregation in schools, whereas the fact is that its thrust was against the institution of slavery. By elaborating the philosophical background of the anti-slavery movement, and repeatedly referring to its broad general purposes, appellants seek to create the impression that segregation in schools was totally at variance with the purposes of that movement. But no amount of argument on a general plane, and no invocation of "ethico-moral-religious-natural rights" (Br. 205) or "Judeo-Christian ethic" (Br. 204) can obscure the fundamental fact that the crusade was directed to the abolition of slavery and not to the objective of setting up mixed schools for white and colored children or enforced commingling of any other kind. The problem before this Court is not the legal or moral justification for slavery; rather, the issue to be resolved is whether the people of the State of South Carolina may, in the exercise of their judgment based on first-hand knowledge of local conditions, decide that the state objective of free public education is best served by a system consisting of separate schools for white and colored children. That question is to be answered in the light of well-settled principles governing the application of the Fourteenth Amendment, and not by general theoretical notions put forward during the antislavery crusade.

Nor is the issue to be resolved on the basis of general statements plucked from their contexts in the debates of Congress or the opinions of this Court. In short, one of the principal fallacies of appellants' brief lies in the fact that it seeks to solve the specific issue of school segregation by addressing itself not to the constitutionality of the practice itself, but rather to broad generalizations.

Another fundamental fallacy in appellants' brief is the assumption that, in the years following the Civil War, the Radical Republicans spoke for Congress as a whole. Nothing could be more misleading. The attitude of Congress towards school segregation during these years must be derived from the action which the Congress as a whole actually took, not only at the time when it proposed the Fourteenth Amendment in 1866, but during the surrounding years. That is the only reliable standard by which to evaluate the opinion of Congress, and the application of that standard shows beyond all peradventure that segregated schooling was not intended to be within the reach of the Fourteenth Amendment – either by the Congress which proposed the Amendment to the States, or by succeeding Congresses.

If we were to adopt the views of the Radical Republicans as representing the views of Congress as a whole, history would have to be rewritten. Surely Congress as a whole did not endorse the vituperative views of Thaddeus Stevens who characterized President Johnson as an "alien enemy, a citizen of a foreign state", or of Charles Sumner who called him "an insolent drunken brute in comparison with which Caligula's horse was respectable". Morison and Commager, 2 *The Growth of the American Republic* 39 (1950).

Still another fundamental fallacy in appellants' argument is the notion that all racial distinctions are "an irrational basis for government action" (Br. 22). The fallacy here has two prongs, the first of which is an apparent effort to smother the fundamental constitutional question by repeated references to "abhorrence of race as a premise for governmental action", "racism", "a state scheme of racism" and the like (Br. 25, 30, 31). This tyranny of words in no way advances resolution of the issue, but rather appears to be an attempt to divert attention from the fundamental constitutional problem at hand, which is to be judged by the application of well-settled principles governing the effect of the Constitution on the police power of the State of South Carolina.

The second prong of this fallacy is appellants' theory that the separate but equal doctrine, as enunciated in *Plessy v. Ferguson*, is an aberration inconsistent with the main stream of cases adjudicated before and since that decision. It is true that *Plessy v. Ferguson* was a case of first impression for the Supreme Court of the United States, so far as the enunciation of the separate but equal doctrine was concerned. But other courts, both State and Federal, had already approved that doctrine long before the Plessy case was decided. The leading decisions on the question had been handed down by the courts of New York, Ohio, Indiana, California and Massachusetts.

We shall more fully explore each of these fallacies and others in appellants' position in answer to the specific questions of the Court.

Robert J. Harris: THE CONSTITUTION, EDUCATION, AND SEGREGATION (Part I)

A . . . possible, but hardly feasible, ground for reversing the "equal but separate" rule might have been found in the historical origins of the fourteenth amendment, the circumstances leading to its adoption and ratification, and the "intentions" of its framers. A wealth of pertinent historical materials had been laboriously presented in briefs and appendices by counsel on reargument. Such a course would have presented a number of obstacles, not the least of which would have been to distinguish between the subjective motivations of the individual members of Congress and the ratifying legislatures and the objective intent of a legislative assembly as a corporate body. For the most part the debates on the fourteenth amendment and on kindred subjects like the Civil Rights and Freedmen's Bureau Bills of 1866, as discussed by counsel, were revealing with respect to the subjective intentions of the active framers (who constituted a minority of the membership of the 39th Congress), but after all it was the fourteenth amendment that was adopted, as Justice Frankfurter has reminded us in another context, and not speeches by its supporters like Representative Bingham and Senator Howard or by its opponents such as Representative Rogers or Senator Garrett Davis.

A second obstacle to having recourse to the intention of the framers is the number and variety of motives back of the adoption of the fourteenth amendment. One intention which the Radicals certainly had, as revealed on the face of the second and third sections, was to make the South and the country safe for the Republican Party by disfranchising the bulk of the southern whites because of their participation in rebellion, by indirectly enfranchising the Negroes, and then establishing governments under the joint control of Negroes, "carpetbaggers," and "scalawags." In this way the Radicals, it was thought, would postpone and perhaps even avoid that day when what Thaddeus Stevens called "yelling secessionists and hissing copperheads" would assume control of the national government. As regards the second and third sections of the Amendment, it is safe to assume that the underlying purpose was not merely to bring about a state of racial equality in the seceding states but to elevate the Negro to a position politically superior to the whites. Intermingled with the realistic and sordid motives underlying these two sections were the noble and idealistic sentiments and aspirations of human equality, individual liberty, and the essential dignity of all men regardless of race or color. These aspirations found expression in the first section in that harmonious unity which emerged from the trinity of privileges and immunities of citizenship, due process of law, and the equal protection of the laws. Finally, there were undoubtedly some who neither understood nor cared about what they were doing so long as they did not run afoul of the Radical leadership or risk political defeat in their home constituencies. All of these factors constitute the most serious hazards in coming to any final conclusion concerning the understanding of the 39th Congress concerning the application of the fourteenth amendment specifically to segregated

From the *Temple Law Quarterly*, Vol. 29, No. 4, Summer, 1956. Reprinted by permission.

education, a subject which was mentioned but hardly discussed.

The course of the proceedings of the Committee of Fifteen on Reconstruction, which drafted the amendment, and the debates in Congress do indicate rather clearly that the final form of the amendment was a compromise phrased with sufficient elasticity to leave a basis for hopes of future fulfillment of present desires by Radicals, Moderates and opponents alike. Actually little of the debate in Congress was spent on the first section of the amendment, and inconclusive as the evidence is upon its specific application, a slight preponderance is perhaps on the side of those who argue that it was not designed to prevent segregated education of its own force. And if action by the ratifying state legislatures is relevant, it is conclusive that a majority of these states understood that the amendment of its own force did not abolish segregation in public education, because they either provided for or retained segregated school systems. Some conclusions, however, can be drawn from the debates in Congress in 1866 and the subsequent discussions leading to the enactment of the Ku Klux Act of 1871 and the Supplementary Civil Rights Act of 1875. First, there appears to have been a subjective intention of a majority of Congressmen and an objective intent of Congress as a corporate body to give to the Negro equality before the law and to strike down state legislation that denied such equality. Second, although the Radicals and Moderates did not preclude judicial enforcement of the fourteenth amendment, they envisaged Congress as the primary and principal organ of enforcement.

These conclusions stem not only from what the 39th and immediately succeeding Congresses said, but more significantly from what they did. From 1866 through 1875 Congress enacted such significant legislation as the Civil Rights Act of 1866, the Ku Klux Act of 1871, and the Supplementary Civil Rights Act of 1875. These acts were designed to remove all legal disqualifications from the Negro in the way of making contracts, suing and testifying in the courts, and owning and disposing of property; to protect the colored race in its exercise of constitutional rights against conspiracies of private citizens; and to afford equal treatment to Negroes in transportation facilities, inns and theaters. Equally significant is what Congress in the ten years after Appomattox did not do. It did not prohibit segregated education in the District of Columbia; it did not deny the admission of Senators and Representatives elected to Congress from those reconstructed states which by law provided for segregation in public schools; and it did not upon the persistent prodding of Sumner and a dwindling band of Radicals extend desegregation to state supported schools or to churches and cemeteries. In all of these deeds of commission and omission Congress spent much time in debating constitutional issues, but in the end the action taken was based upon a shrewd conception of politics as the art of the possible rather than upon convictions founded on constitutional law. In all of these actions, too, the majority in Congress placed no serious reliance upon the judiciary to enforce the provisions of the fourteenth amendment. The Democrats and Conservative Republicans were left with the task of opposing implementing legislation as unnecessary on the ground that the amendment was self-executing and all that was needed was investing the courts with jurisdiction to enforce the laws. The Radicals and some of the Moderates did not trust the Supreme Court. After all it had infuriated them by its decision in the *Milligan* case and by merely entertaining suits to challenge the validity of the Reconstruction Act in *Mississippi v. Johnson* and *Georgia v. Stanton.* Republican distrust of the Court as an agency of government, particularly with respect to the administration of reconstruction policy, of which the fourteenth amendment was an integral part, is reflected in congressional criticism of the Court, bills to curtail the exercise of judicial review, and the act withdrawing appellate jurisdiction from the Court in specified cases designed to prevent a decision upon the validity of reconstruction policy in *Ex parte McCardle,* although the case already had been heard and a conference on its disposition held. In failing to rely upon judicial enforcement the Republican majority did not, to be sure, preclude its possibility; the failure merely emphasized their conception of Congress as the principal instrumentality to enforce the amendment and reflected their distrust of the Court as it was then constituted. . . .

BROWN *et al. v.* BOARD OF EDUCATION OF TOPEKA *et al.*

Mr. Chief Justice Warren delivered the opinion of the Court.

THESE cases come to us from the States of Kansas, South Carolina, Virginia, and Delaware. They are premised on different facts and different local conditions, but a common legal question justifies their consideration together in this consolidated opinion.

In each of the cases, minors of the Negro race, through their legal representatives, seek the aid of the courts in obtaining admission to the public schools of their community on a nonsegregated basis. In each instance, they had been denied admission to schools attended by white children under laws requiring or permitting segregation according to race. This segregation was alleged to deprive the plaintiffs of the equal protection of the laws under the Fourteenth Amendment. In each of the cases other than the Delaware case, a three-judge federal district court denied relief to the plaintiffs on the so-called "separate but equal" doctrine announced by this Court in *Plessy v. Ferguson,* 163 U.S. 537. Under that doctrine, equality of treatment is accorded when the races are provided substantially equal facilities, even though these facilities be separate. In the Delaware case, the Supreme Court of Delaware adhered to that doctrine, but ordered that the plaintiffs be admitted to the white schools because of their superiority to the Negro schools.

The plaintiffs contend that segregated public schools are not "equal" and cannot be made "equal," and that hence they are deprived of the equal protection of the laws. Because of the obvious importance of the question presented, the Court took jurisdiction. Argument was heard in the 1952 Term, and reargument was heard this Term on certain questions propounded by the Court.

Reargument was largely devoted to the circumstances surrounding the adoption of the Fourteenth Amendment in 1868. It covered exhaustively consideration of the Amendment in Congress, ratification by the states, then existing prac-

347 U.S. 483 [1953]

tices in racial segregation, and the views of proponents and opponents of the Amendment. This discussion and our own investigation convince us that, although these sources cast some light, it is not enough to resolve the problem with which we are faced. At best, they are inconclusive. The most avid proponents of the post-War Amendments undoubtedly intended them to remove all legal distinctions among "all persons born or naturalized in the United States." Their opponents, just as certainly, were antagonistic to both the letter and the spirit of the Amendments and wished them to have the most limited effect. What others in Congress and the state legislatures had in mind cannot be determined with any degree of certainty.

An additional reason for the inconclusive nature of the Amendment's history, with respect to segregated schools, is the status of public education at that time. In the South, the movement toward free common schools, supported by general taxation, had not yet taken hold. Education of white children was largely in the hands of private groups. Education of Negroes was almost nonexistent, and practically all of the race were illiterate. In fact, any education of Negroes was forbidden by law in some states. Today, in contrast, many Negroes have achieved outstanding success in the arts and sciences as well as in the business and professional world. It is true that public school education at the time of the Amendment had advanced further in the North, but the effect of the Amendment on Northern States was generally ignored in the congressional debates. Even in the North, the conditions of public education did not approximate those existing today. The curriculum was usually rudimentary; ungraded schools were common in rural areas; the school term was but three months a year in many states; and compulsory school attendance was virtually unknown. As a consequence, it is not surprising that there should be so little in the history of the Fourteenth Amendment relating to its intended effect on public education.

In the first cases in this Court construing the Fourteenth Amendment, decided shortly after its adoption, the Court interpreted it as proscribing all state-imposed discriminations against the Negro race. The doctrine of "separate but equal" did not make its appearance in this Court until 1896 in the case of *Plessy v. Ferguson, supra,* involving not education but transportation. American courts have since labored with the doctrine for over half a century. In this Court, there have been six cases involving the "separate but equal" doctrine in the field of public education. In *Cumming v. County Board of Education,* 175 U.S. 528, and *Gong Lum v. Rice,* 275 U.S. 78, the validity of the doctrine itself was not challenged. In more recent cases, all on the graduate school level, inequality was found in that specific benefits enjoyed by white students were denied to Negro students of the same educational qualifications. *Missouri ex rel. Gaines v. Canada,* 305 U.S. 337; *Sipuel v. Oklahoma,* 332 U.S. 631; *Sweatt v. Painter,* 339 U.S. 629; *McLaurin v. Oklahoma State Regents,* 339 U.S. 637. In none of these cases was it necessary to re-examine the doctrine to grant relief to the Negro plaintiff. And in *Sweatt v. Painter, supra,* the Court expressly reserved decision on the question whether *Plessy v. Ferguson* should be held inapplicable to public education.

In the instant cases, that question is directly presented. Here, unlike *Sweatt v. Painter,* there are findings below that the Negro and white schools involved have been equalized, or are being equalized, with respect to buildings, curricula, qualifications and salaries of teachers, and other "tangible" factors. Our decision, therefore, cannot turn on merely a comparison of these tangible factors in the Negro and white schools involved in each of the cases. We must look instead to the effect of segregation itself on public education.

In approaching this problem, we cannot turn the clock back to 1868 when the Amendment was adopted, or even to 1896 when *Plessy v. Ferguson* was written. We must consider public education in the light of its full development and its present place in American life throughout the Nation. Only in this way can it be determined if segregation in public schools deprives these plaintiffs of the equal protection of the laws.

Today, education is perhaps the most important function of state and local governments. Compulsory school attendance laws and the great expenditures for education both demonstrate our recognition of the importance of education to our democratic society. It is required in the performance of our most basic public responsibilities, even service in the armed forces. It is the very foundation of good citizenship. Today it is a principal instrument in awakening the child to cultural values, in preparing him for later professional training, and in helping him to adjust normally to his environment. In these days, it is doubtful that any child may reasonably be expected to succeed in life if he is denied the opportunity of an education. Such an opportunity, where the state has undertaken to provide it, is a right which must be made available to all on equal terms.

We come then to the question presented: Does segregation of children in public schools solely on the basis of race, even though the physical facilities and other "tangible" factors may be equal, deprive the children of the minority group of equal educational opportunities? We believe that it does.

In *Sweatt v. Painter, supra,* in finding that a segregated law school for Negroes could not provide them equal educational opportunities, this Court relied in large part on "those qualities which are incapable of objective measurement but which make for greatness in a law school." In *McLaurin v. Oklahoma State Regents, supra,* the Court, in requiring that a Negro admitted to a white graduate school be treated like all other students, again resorted to intangible considerations: ". . . his ability to study, to engage in discussions and exchange views with other students, and, in general, to learn his profession." Such considerations apply with added force to children in grade and high schools. To separate them from others of similar age and qualifications solely because of their race generates a feeling of inferiority as to their status in the community that may affect their hearts and minds in a way unlikely ever to be undone. The effect of this separation on their educational opportunities was well stated by a finding in the Kansas case by a court which nevertheless felt compelled to rule against the Negro plaintiffs:

> Segregation of white and colored children in public schools has a detrimental effect upon the colored children. The impact is greater when it has the sanction of the law; for the policy of separating the races is usually interpreted as denoting the inferiority of the negro group. A sense of inferiority affects the motivation of a child to learn. Segregation with the sanction of law, therefore, has a tendency to [retard] the education and mental development of negro children and

to deprive them of some of the benefits they would receive in a racial[ly] integrated school system.[1]

Whatever may have been the extent of psychological knowledge at the time of *Plessy v. Ferguson*, this finding is amply supported by modern authority. Any language in *Plessy v. Ferguson* contrary to this finding is rejected.[2]

We conclude that in the field of public education the doctrine of "separate but equal" has no place. Separate educational facilities are inherently unequal. Therefore, we hold that the plaintiffs and others similarly situated for whom the actions have been brought are, by reason of the segregation complained of, deprived of the equal protection of the laws guaranteed by the Fourteenth Amendment. This disposition makes unnecessary any discussion whether such segregation also violates the Due Process Clause of the Fourteenth Amendment.

Because these are class actions, because of the wide applicability of this decision, and because of the great variety of local conditions, the formulation of decrees in these cases presents problems of considerable complexity. On reargument, the consideration of appropriate relief was necessarily subordinated to the primary question — the constitutionality of segregation on public education. We have now announced that such segregation is a denial of the equal protection of the laws. In order that we may have the full assistance of the parties in formulating decrees, the cases will be restored to the docket, and the parties are requested to present further argument on Questions 4 and 5 previously propounded by the Court for the reargument this Term. The Attorney General of the United States is again invited to participate. The Attorneys General of the states requiring or permitting segregation in public education will also be permitted to appear as *Amici Curiae* upon request,

[1] [But another lower court stated, among other things, that: "To this we may add that, when seventeen states and the Congress of the United States have for more than three-quarters of a century required segregation of the races in the public schools, and when this has received the approval of the leading appelate courts of the country including the unanimous approval of the Supreme Court of the United States (in *Gong Lum v. Rice,*) at a time when that court included Chief Justice Taft and Justices Stone, Holmes, and Brandeis, it is a late day to say that such segregation is violative of fundamental constitutional rights. It is hardly reasonable to suppose that legislative bodies over so wide a territory, including the Congress of the United States, and great judges of high courts have knowingly defied the Constitution for so long a period or that they have acted in ignorance of the meaning of its provisions. The constitution principle is the same now that it has been throughout this period; and if conditions have changed so that segregation is no longer wise, this is a matter for the legislatures and not for the courts. The members of the judiciary have no more right to read their ideas of sociology into the Constitution than their ideas of economics." 98 F. Supp. 529, at 537. ED.]

[2] [On February 25, 1957, the Supreme Court handed down its decision in *Radovich v. National Football League*, in which it held that professional football was subject to the anti-trust laws while professional baseball was not. Mr. Justice Clark, speaking for the majority said, among other things: "If this ruling is unrealistic, inconsistent, or illogical, it is sufficient to answer — that were we considering the question of baseball for the first time upon a clean slate we would have no doubts — We, therefore, conclude that the orderly way to eliminate error or discrimination, if any there be, is by legislation and not by court decision. Congressional processes are more accommodative, affording the whole industry hearings and an opportunity to assist in the formulation of new legislation. The resulting product is therefore more likely to protect the industry and the public alike. The whole scope of Congressional action would be known in advance and effective dates for the legislation could be set in the future without the injustices of retroactivity and surprise which might follow court action." ED.]

to do so by September 15, 1954, and submission of briefs by October 1, 1954.[3]

[3] [The question of relief was argued on April 11–14, 1955. On May 31, 1955, the Supreme Court (349 U.S. 294 [1955]) issued its order as follows: "These cases were (originally) decided on May 17, 1954. The opinions of that date, declaring the fundamental principle that racial discrimination in public education is unconstitutional, are incorporated herein – All provision of federal, state or local law requiring or permitting such discrimination must yield to this principle – Full implementation of these Constitutional principles may require solution of varied local school problems. School authorities have the primary responsibility for elucidating, assessing, and solving these problems; courts will have to consider whether the action of school authorities constitutes good faith – Because of their proximity to local conditions and the possible need for further hearings courts which originally heard these cases can best perform this judicial appraisal. Accordingly, we – remand these cases to those courts. In fashioning and effectuating the decrees, the courts will be guided by equitable principles –. But it should go without saying that the vitality of these constitutional principles cannot be allowed to yield simply because of disagreement with them. – The Courts will require – a prompt and reasonable start toward full compliance – and enter such orders and decrees – as are necessary and proper to admit to public schools on a socially non-discriminating basis with all deliberate speed the parties to these cases. . . ." ED.]

BOLLING *et al. v.* SHARPE *et al.*

Mr. Chief Justice Warren delivered the opinion of the Court

THIS case challenges the validity of segregation in the public schools of the District of Columbia. The petitioners, minors of the Negro race, allege that such segregation deprives them of due process of law under the Fifth Amendment. They were refused admission to a public school attended by white children solely because of their race. They sought the aid of the District Court for the District of Columbia in obtaining admission. That court dismissed their complaint. The Court granted a writ of certiorari before judgment in the Court of Appeals because of the importance of the constitutional question presented. 344 U. S. 873

We have this day held that the Equal Protection Clause of the Fourteenth Amendment prohibits the states from maintaining racially segregated public schools. The legal problem in the District of Columbia is somewhat different, however. The Fifth Amendment, which is applicable in the District of Columbia, does not contain an equal protection clause as does the Fourteenth Amendment which applies only to the states. But the concepts of equal protection and due process, both stemming from our American ideal of fairness, are not mutually exclusive. The "equal protection of the laws" is a more explicit safeguard of prohibited unfairness than "due process of law", and, therefore, we do not imply that the two are always interchangeable phrases. But, as this Court has recognized, discrimination may be so unjustifiable as to be violative of due process.

Classifications based solely upon race must be scrutinized with particular care since they are contrary to our traditions and hence constitutionally suspect. As long ago as 1896, this Court declared the principle "that the Constitution of the United States, in its present form, forbids, so far as civil and political rights are concerned, discrimination by the General Government, or by the States, against any citizen because of his race." And in

347 U.S. 497 [1953]

Buchanan v. Warley, 245 U. S. 60, the Court held that a statute which limited the right of a property owner to convey his property to a person of another race was, as an unreasonable discrimination, a denial of due process of law.

Although the Court has not assumed to define "liberty" with any great precision, that term is not confined to mere freedom from bodily restraint. Liberty under the law extends to the full range of conduct which the individual is free to pursue, and it cannot be restricted except for a proper governmental objective. Segregation in public education is not reasonably related to any proper governmental objective, and thus it imposes on Negro children of the District of Columbia a burden that constitutes an arbitrary deprivation of their liberty in violation of the Due Process Clause.

In view of our decision that the Constitution prohibits the states from maintaining racially segregated public schools, it would be unthinkable that the same Constitution would impose a lesser duty on the Federal Government. We hold that racial segregation in the public schools of the District of Columbia is a denial of the due process of law guaranteed by the Fifth Amendment to the Constitution.

For the reasons set out in *Brown v. Board of Education,* this case will be restored to the docket for reargument on Questions 4 and 5 previously propounded by the Court. 345 U. S. 972

It is so ordered

COMMONWEALTH OF PENNSYLVANIA, CITY OF PHILADELPHIA, *et al., appellants, v.* THE BOARD OF DIRECTORS OF CITY TRUSTS OF CITY OF PHILADELPHIA

PROCEEDING for citation to Philadelphia Board of Directors of City Trusts to show cause why certain Negro applicants should not be admitted to school which was administered by the Board as trustee and which had been established pursuant to will providing that it should be operated for white male orphans. From a decree of the Orphans' Court of Philadelphia affirming the Board's refusal of applications for admission and dismissing petitions for citation, appeals were taken. The Supreme Court of Pennsylvania, 386 Pa. 548, 127 A. 2d 287, affirmed and an appeal was taken. The Supreme Court treated the papers whereon the appeal was taken as a petition for certiorari and held that, in view of fact that Philadelphia Board of Directors of City Trusts is an agency of the State of Pennsylvania, its action in denying applicants admission merely because they were Negroes was discrimination by the State, forbidden by the Fourteenth Amendment of the United States Constitution.

* * *

PER CURIAM

(1) The motion to dismiss the appeal for want of jurisdiction is granted. . . . Treating the papers whereon the appeal was taken as a petition for writ of certiorari, . . . the petition is granted. . . . Stephen Girard, by a will probated in 1831, left a fund in trust for the erection, maintenance, and operation of a "college." The will provided that the college

No. 769. Decided April 29, 1957. (Vol. 77, Supreme Court Reporter, 806.)

was to admit "as many poor white male orphans, between the ages of six and ten years, as the said income shall be adequate to maintain." The will named as trustee the City of Philadelphia. The provisions of the will were carried out by the State and city and the college was opened in 1848. Since 1869, by virtue of an act of the Pennsylvania Legislature, the trust has been administered and the college operated by the "Board of Directors of City Trusts of the City of Philadelphia." . . .

(2) In February, 1954, the petitioners Foust and Felder applied for admission to the college. They met all qualifications except that they were Negroes. For this reason the Board refused to admit them. They petitioned the Orphan's Court of Philadelphia County for an order directing the Board to admit them, alleging that their exclusion because of race violated the Fourteenth Amendment to the Constitution. The State of Pennsylvania and the City of Philadelphia joined in the suit also contending the Board's action violated the Fourteenth Amendment. The Orphan's Court rejected the constitutional contention and refused to order the applicants' admission. . . . This was affirmed by the Pennsylvania Supreme Court. 386 Pa. 548, 127 A.2d 287.

The Board which operates Girard College is an agency of the State of Pennsylvania. Therefore, even though the Board was acting as a trustee, its refusal to admit Foust and Felder to the college because they were Negroes was discrimination by the State. Such discrimination is forbidden by the Fourteenth Amendment. *Brown v. Board of Education*, 347, U. S. 483, 74 S.Ct. 686, 98 L.Ed. 873. Accordingly, the judgment of the Supreme Court of Pennsylvania is reversed and the cause is remanded for further proceedings not inconsistent with this opinion.

Reversed and remanded with directions.

Robert J. Harris: THE CONSTITUTION, EDUCATION, AND SEGREGATION (Part II)

SELDOM, if ever, has the Supreme Court of the United States reversed an earlier decision without finding either that the case was erroneously decided at the time of decision on the basis of conflict with history or of inconsistency with then existing precedent, or concluding that the case has not been followed subsequently and is indeed in conflict with later decisions. The Court has never been more candid in basing a reversal of precedent on changing conditions and new developments alone than it was here. The Court at no place said that *Plessy v. Ferguson* was erroneously decided in 1896. Indeed the implication is that *Plessy v. Ferguson* had become bad because of the growth of public education from the crude and precarious thing it was in 1868 and 1896 into the all-encompassing and grandiose thing it had become by 1954, and because of advances in psychological knowledge. By now, of course, it is no longer a novelty for the Court to reverse its earlier decisions or even to advance the concept of adapting the law to meet changes in social conditions, but it is a rarity to the point of novelty for the Court to do either completely outside the framework of history

From the *Temple Law Quarterly*, Vol. 29, No. 4, Summer, 1956. Reprinted by permission.

or of litigated cases decided either previously or subsequently. And, . . . it was unnecessary for the Court to do so here. All it had to do was to hold that the "equal but separate" formula when applied by a state or its officials was not in accord with precedents before and after 1896, and that accordingly *Plessy v. Ferguson* was reversed. Such a course would have combined both the concept of constitutional growth through judicial interpretation and an adherence to precedent in the orderly development of the organic law, and it would have rendered the Court less vulnerable to criticisms to the effect that the decision was sheer judicial legislation.

By all standards, however, the *decision* in the *Segregation Cases* was a great decision. The *opinion,* on the other hand, was not a great opinion. Indeed, after the exhaustive records compiled and the elaborate arguments adduced in briefs and supplements of counsel, the opinion was something of an anticlimax and did not reach "the height of this great argument" to assert equality before the law and to justify the ways of the law to man. Moreover, the Court's opinion lacked the vigor and conviction of the dissents of the first Justice Harlan in other cases dealing with segregation, and it fell short of the legal craftsmanship of more recent opinions by Chief Justice Hughes, Justice Cardozo, and Justice Stone which changed the course of the law by reversing earlier decisions. However, despite its deficiencies in rhetoric and craftsmanship, the opinion is still in the great tradition of constitutional growth by judicial interpretation initiated by Chief Justice Marshall and continued by such illustrious successors as Justice Holmes whose words are as applicable to the fourteenth amendment as to the Constitution it changed. Justice Holmes said:

> When we are dealing with words that also are a constituent act, like the Constitution of the United States, we must realize that they have called into life a being the development of which could not have been foreseen completely by the most gifted of its begetters.
> . The Case before us must be considered in the light of our whole experience, and not merely in that of what was said a hundred years ago.

This is what Chief Justice Warren must have had in mind in his reference to the great changes in public education and his assertion that we cannot turn the clock back to 1868 or even to 1896. Much has happened to the Negro, to education, and to the Constitution which could not have been foreseen by Thaddeus Stevens or Jacob Howard. Not the least of what has occurred has been the atrophy of the fifth section of the fourteenth amendment as a result both of judicial decisions and of the continuing influence of John C. Calhoun, whose mischievous device of the concurrent veto finds current expression in the senate filibuster and the seniority rule in the organization of congressional committees either of which is a sufficient barrier to legislative implementation of the fourteenth amendment. If the fourteenth amendment is to have meaning, the Court must provide it, and in doing so it must have regard to all relevant factors. The decision of the Court in the *Segregation Cases* by looking upon the Constitution as a process of growth, and by bringing constitutional interpretation nearer to the American ideal of the equality of all men in the enjoyment of legal privileges and immunities, is bound to occupy a prominent place in constitutional history long after analysts have ceased to write about it and the strident voices of neo-nullificationists have been stilled. . . .

Paul A. Freund: UNDERSTANDING THE SCHOOL DECISION

UNANIMOUS decisions of the Supreme Court are uncommon enough in ordinary cases, and especially rare in extraordinary ones. When, therefore, the unanimous decision in the school segregation cases provokes attacks on the Court for "judicial usurpation" and "naked judicial power," the lines of communication between the Court and the people have been badly tangled. The phrases just quoted are taken from the Declaration of Constitutional Principles issued by 19 Senators and 81 representatives in the United States Congress.

This declaration (popularly known as the Southern manifesto) is only the latest and most dramatic item of evidence that we may be facing not only a crisis in race relations but – what could in the long run be even more shattering – a crisis in the role of the Supreme Court as the authoritative voice of our highest law. The latter threat, no less than the former, calls for the fullest possible measure of understanding.

One thing can surely be said of the segregation cases: They were not hastily or thoughtlessly decided. Every contention now advanced against the decision was presented to the Court in briefs, running to hundreds of pages, and in oral argument. The Court was exceptionally deliberate in its treatment of this litigation. The cases were originally set for argument in October 1952. Argument was postponed by the Court until December. In June 1953, the Court ordered the cases reargued at the following term, specifying certain questions, including historical inquiries, to be canvassed by counsel.

In December 1953 the reargument took place. The Court was assisted not only by the unusually thorough briefs of the complainants and the defendant States but by a full-scale brief submitted by Attorney General Brownell, in support of the complainants' position. On May 17, 1954, the decision was finally handed down; but even then the Court avoided precipitate action. Still another argument was ordered on the question of the form of relief.

The attorneys general of all States requiring or permitting racial discrimination in public education were invited to present their views, and the representatives of six states – Florida, North Carolina, Arkansas, Oklahoma, Maryland, and Texas – were in fact heard, in addition to the States directly involved in the cases – Kansas, South Carolina, Virginia, Delaware, and the District of Columbia.

The judgment of the Court was announced on May 31, 1955, more than 3 years after the cases had been docketed there, and after every forewarning that a momentous decision might be forthcoming, but still with forbearance in the order for enforcement. The NAACP had asked for decrees effective not later than the opening of the next school year. The Attorney General's brief had suggested decrees requiring plans to be submitted by the States within 90 days, "for ending, as soon as possible, racial segregation of pupils in public schools.

The Court took the more moderate course of directing the lower courts to enter "such orders and decrees consistent with this opinion as are necessary and proper to admit to public schools on a

Reprinted by permission of Paul A. Freund, Charles Stebbins Fairchild professor of law of the Harvard Law School from *The Christian Science Monitor*, March 26, 27, 1956, and *Congressional Record*, March 28, 1956.

racially nondiscriminatory basis with all deliberate speed the parties to these cases." The phrase "deliberate speed" is a term of legal art deriving from 18th century chancery practice, and not, as certain litterateurs surmised, from the haunting refrain in Francis Thomson's religious poem The Hound of Heaven: "Deliberate speed, majestic instancy."

The literary reference does, however, serve by contrast to underscore the judicious restraint shown by the Court. Majestic instancy would have been too heroic a demand for mortal men faced with genuine problems of school districting allotment of pupils, and similar administrative burdens. Nevertheless the opinion made it plain that delay for reasons of community nonacceptance would not be legitimate. "But it should go without saying," the opinion of Chief Justice Warren declared, "that the vitality of these constitutional principles cannot be allowed to yield simply because of disagreement with them."

Those who disagree with the decision on constitutional grounds argue that it is not justified by either the language or the history of the 14th amendment. The Congressmen's declaration, for example, states: "The original Constitution does not mention education. Neither does the 14th Amendment nor any other amendment."

This, of course, is true. The 14th Amendment provides that "No State shall make or enforce any law which shall abridge the privileges or immunities of citizens of the United States; nor shall any State deprive any person of life, liberty, or property, without due process of law; nor deny to any person the equal protection of the laws."

But the argument from the silence of the Constitution about education proves much too much. It is the very essence of the Constitution that it speaks in generalities like "equal protection of the laws," and it is the very essence of the judicial process that it must apply the generalities to the concrete facts of experience. Nowhere does the Constitution mention agriculture; are there then literalists who would conclude that Congress is out of bounds in debating Federal price supports for agricultural commodities?

Note, too, that the argument from the silence of the Constitution would rule out any Federal standard whatever for public education, the separate-but-equal standard no less than desegregation. In this respect the declaration is not free from ambiguity, for it quotes with apparent approval the separate-but-equal doctrine as an "established legal principle almost a century old." It is not clear, that is, whether the usurpation by the court is thought to begin when any facilities at all are required for the public education of Negroes, or equal facilities in separate schools, or admission without regard to race.

The argument from the historical background, rather than the text, of the 14th amendment, is subtler, and it leads to some basic questions about the nature of constitutional interpretation. To quote once more the declaration of the Members of Congress: "The debates preceding the submission of the 14th amendment clearly show that there was no intent that it should affect the systems of education maintained by the States."

Here there is further ambiguity. If the meaning is that there was no specific, calculated purpose to deal with education, the statement is undoubtedly true. If the meaning is that there was a specific, calculated purpose to exclude education, the debates are plainer to the signers of the Declaration than they were to the Court or to the Attorney General. The word used by Chief Justice Warren to describe the debates is "inconclusive." This is hardly surprising, in view of the relatively minor role of public education at the time, and the correspondingly fragmentary attention it received in the spacious discussions in Congress over privileges and immunities of citizens and equal protection of the laws.

Most schooling in the South was private in 1868; for Negroes it was virtually non-existent there; and throughout the country the public-school system and compulsory education as we know it were in a rudimentary stage. The Congress which approved the 14th amendment did not forsee the development in education which has taken place and did not foreclose the participation by Negroes in that development on a plane of equality, for equal protection of the laws was adopted as a standard without exceptions or exemptions.

Even if the legislative history had shown more evidence than it did of an intention not to cover public education, the interpretation of the 14th amendment would not necessarily be circumscribed by that sentiment. The Founding Fathers in the convention of 1787 voted down a proposal to authorize Congress to grant charters of incorporation. This negative vote did not later prevent such charters from being granted and upheld, under general language which the framers approved.

Very often, and very properly, the real intention of constitutional assemblies is to establish principles and to leave the hard questions of their application to be worked out in the unknown future. Thereby trouble is not borrowed for the present, and the unfolding life of the future is not strait-jacketed.

The process is misunderstood if it is thought to be peculiar to the 14th amendment. The sixth amendment, for example, provides that "the accused shall enjoy the right . . . to have the assistance of counsel for his defense." When this was formulated in 1789, the right of an accused person was denied in England for many types of crimes; not until 1836 was that right fully granted in England.

With us, however, the guarantee has come to mean more than the right to have the assistance of counsel who is employed. It has come to mean, as interpreted by the Supreme Court, the right of an indigent defendant to have counsel appointed for him by the trial court. This is simply an illustration of Chief Justice Hughes' pronouncement in the famous mortgage moratorium case in 1934:

> It is no answer to say that this public need was not apprehended a century ago, or to insist that was what the provision of the Constitution meant to the vision of our time. If by the statement that what the Constitution meant at the time of its adoption it means today, it is intended to say that the great clauses of the Constitution must be confined to the interpretation which the framers, with the conditions and outlook of their time, would have placed upon them, the statement carries its own refutation. . . .

Is there, then, no criterion of meaning for the general guarantees of the Constitution? Must the Justices do what they are accused of doing in the Congressmen's declaration, substituting personal, political, and social ideas for the established law of the land?

The answer is that as the function of a Justice is necessarily something more than to be a grammarian, it is decidedly less than to be a zealot. The Court interprets to us our own ideals implanted in the constitutional document, as they have flowered in our national life. Justice Holmes put a complex idea concisely in speaking of the provisions of the Constitution; "Their significance is not formal: it is to be gathered not simply by taking the words and a dictionary, but by considering their origin and the line of their growth."

"The line of their growth" is a key to the understanding of the segregation cases. Whatever the purposes the 14th amendment may serve – and it has come to serve a good many collateral ones, such as the rule of "1 thing, 1 tax" in state taxation – its basic aim concerned equality of rights for Negroes. The development of that concept is a story of successive applications of the principle to a widening variety of practices.

In 1880 the right to be included on juries was established. In 1917 racial restrictions in zoning laws were held invalid, despite the argument of the municipality that property values and public order required the discrimination.

In 1927 the all-white primary election was ruled invalid, despite the argument of the State that primaries are a private political affair. In a passage resembling some current protests, the brief of the State of Texas declared, "It must be remembered that nominating primaries were unknown at the time of the adoption of the Constitution of the United States and of the constitution of Texas in 1876. The question of parties and their regulation is a political one rather than legal."

Then in 1938 a Negro applicant was ordered admitted to the law school of the University of Missouri, despite the State's offer to pay his tuition at a nondiscriminating law school in a neighboring State. Since Missouri had no separate (and equal) law school for Negroes, the color line had to be broken in the State university. Mr. Justice McReynolds, who dissented from the opinion delivered by Chief Justice Hughes, saw clearly enough the line of growth in education, and he did not like it. He said:

> For a long time Missouri has acted upon the view that the best interest of her people demands separation of whites and Negroes in schools. Under the opinion just announced, I presume she may abandon her law school and thereby disadvantage her white citizens without impairing petitioner's opportunities for legal instruction; or she may break down the settled practice concerning separate schools and thereby, as indicated by experience, damnify both races.

All of these cases had their sequels, in which the Court turned back attempts to circumvent the decisions or to blunt their effect by differentiating them from cases coming before the courts. Much of the progress was made before World War II. Since then, in Korea and in military posts around the globe, as well as at home, we have extended the principle of desegregation. The question before the Court in the school cases was whether the vital growth had come to an end in the educational sphere with the separate-but-equal doctrine or whether it carried through to desegregation.

The Court could have answered in any of three ways. It could have answered as it did, finding that the principle of equality was not exhausted by separate but equal facilities; that as a Nation we had moved beyond that stage in profession and to a substantial degree in practice; and that the real and painful difficulties of adjustment in certain areas would be given proper respect by allowing time for administrative change-overs.

The second possible choice for the Court would have been to leave the matter to Congress under the power to enforce the provisions of the 14th amendment. That course would have been the easiest for the Court to take, but it would not have been the most straightforward.

The advances already made in applying the principle of equality had been achieved through resort to the Court, not to Congress: zoning, primaries, university education. Congress was not in the habit of taking responsibility in this field, or indeed in any of the other ramifications of the 14th amendment as limits on the powers of the States. To have dropped the issue in the lap of Congress would have been extraordinary. Congress, on its part, could have been expected to regard the issue as a judicial one and to play an Alphonse-Gaston game.

The third possibility was to decide that education is not included in the guarantee of equal protection of the laws, or that the guarantee is satisfied by separate public schooling. This would have been a pronouncement that as a people we do not recognize fellowship in the educational process to be a minimum standard for governments to observe in our common life, that the vital growth of the principle of equality has not carried to this point.

Would we have been satisfied with this reflection of our own better nature as a people? For it is just that better nature which we mean the Court to hold up to us in interpreting the Bill of Rights. A philosopher, Alexander Meiklejohn, once described the Court's function in this way:

> That Court is commissioned to interpret to us our own purposes, our own meaning . . . And its teaching has peculiar importance because it interprets principles of fact and of value, not merely in the abstract, but also in their bearing upon the concrete immediate problems which are, at any given moment, puzzling and dividing us.

If the Court was wrong in the school cases it is because the Court misjudged our present-day ideal of equality in law. To judge the decision, therefore, is to judge ourselves, all of us, for the Constitution sets a common, not a sectional, standard for the country. That is why it is supremely important, too, that those who believe the Court judged rightly, as well as the critics, should let their voices be heard.

Ralph T. Catterall: JUDICIAL SELF-RESTRAINT: THE OBLIGATION OF THE JUDICIARY

IN his address at the John Marshall Bicentennial Ceremonies, 41 A.B.A.J. 1009, Chief Justice Warren said:

> Insistence upon the independence of the judiciary in the early days of our nation was perhaps John Marshall's greatest contribution to constitutional law. He aptly stated the controlling principle when, in speaking of the Court during his tenure, he said that they had "never sought to enlarge the judicial power beyond its proper bounds, nor feared to carry it to the fullest extent that duty required." That is precisely the obligation of the judiciary today. Self-restraint and fearlessness are always essential attributes of every branch of our Government.

An independent judiciary (with power to issue a writ of habeas corpus) marks the dividing line between a free nation and a police state. A police state is a

Ralph T. Catterall, "Judicial Self-Restraint: The Obligation of the Judiciary," *American Bar Association Journal*, September, 1956, Vol. 42, No. 9, pp. 829–833. Reprinted by permission.

state where the police can hold you in custody as long as they please, and no judge who is not himself afraid of the police can let you out. So the Act of Settlement, 1701, settled the British Crown on the Protestant descendants of the Electress Sophia on condition that they appoint judges for life; our own Declaration of Independence denounced George III for not extending that principle to the Colonies ("He made Judges dependent on his Will alone, for the tenure of their offices, and the amount and payment of their salaries."); and the Constitution of the United States embodies that principle. We cannot get along without it. It is a pearl of great price. The great price that the people willingly pay to have judges who are not dependent on anybody is that everybody is dependent on the self-restraint of the judges. To them we confide the power to make decisions affecting life, liberty and property in return for their promise to apply the law as they honestly understand it.

Dissenting in *United States v. Butler*, 297 U. S. 1 (1936), complaining of the abuse of judicial power and "a tortured construction of the Constitution," Mr. Justice Stone said (page 78):

> The power of courts to declare a statute unconstitutional is subject to two guiding principles of decision which ought never to be absent from judicial consciousness. One is that courts are concerned only with the power to enact statutes, not with their wisdom. The other is that while unconstitutional exercise of power by the executive and legislative branches of the government is subject to judicial restraint, the only check upon our own exercise of power is our own sense of self-restraint.

Those words rankled in the breast of Mr. Justice Sutherland for months. To him they seemed to "offend the proprieties" and "impugn the good faith of those who think otherwise." So, dissenting in *West Coast Hotel Co. v. Parrish,* 300 U. S. 379 (1937), he unburdened himself (page 402):

> The suggestion that the only check upon the exercise of the judicial power, when properly invoked, to declare a constitutional right superior to an unconstitutional statute is the judge's own faculty of self-restraint, is both ill considered and mischievous. Self-restraint belongs in the domain of will and not of judgment. The check upon the judge is that imposed by his oath of office, by the Constitution and by his own conscientious and informed convictions; and since he has the duty to make up his own mind and adjudge accordingly, it is hard to see how there could be any other restraint.

Justice Sutherland was quite right in saying that "self-restraint belongs in the domain of will and not of judgment." It calls for enough will power to resist the temptation to do good. ("Good" in this context means what the judge knows is good. ["Knows" means what the judge knows that he knows.]) Whether, in a given case, the judge will ignore the written law that he has promised to obey in favor of his concept of natural law depends on the strength of his convictions. He will do so only when he knows that he is right. Justice Holmes was sceptical about natural law for the same reason that he distrusted the man who knows he is right.

Chief Justice Marshall had convictions about the sanctity of the ownership of land. He had gone deeply in debt to buy land in the Northern Neck of Virginia, and Virginia had passed a statute the effect of which, if valid, would be to deprive him of his land.

Fletcher v. Peck, 6 Cranch 87 (1810), involved a Georgia statute that deprived landowners of their land. That was before the Fourteenth Amendment; and the due process clause in the Bill of Rights did not apply to the states. Marshall held that the Georgia statute violated the contract clause of the Federal Constitution. But for good measure he held as an independent and sufficient ground for his judgment that the statute was void as a matter of natural law (page 139):

> . . . the State of Georgia was restrained either by general principles which are common to our free institutions, or by the particular provisions of the Constitution of the United States, from passing a law. . . .

He takes his stand that a state law is void in two separate instances: (1) if it violates the Constitution, and (2) if it violates general principles.

Mr. Justice William Johnson, Jefferson's first appointee to the Court, could not go along with Marshall on the constitutional ground. He said (page 143):

> I do not hesitate to declare that a state does not possess the power of revoking its own grants. But I do it on a general principle, on the reason and nature of things: a principle which will impose laws even on the Deity.

Judge Johnson knows he is right even if the Deity should differ with him. Most supporters of natural law are more modest: they are merely certain that *they* know the Laws of Nature and of Nature's God.

Loan Association v. Topeka, 20 Wall. 655 (1875), held a state statute void on general principles. The Court did not rely on or mention any clause of the Constitution. The Fourteenth Amendment had been on the books for seven years, but the Justices had not yet discovered the talismanic properties of the due process clause. To Mr. Justice Miller the statute looked like robbery, and that was all he needed to know. He said (page 664):

> To lay, with one hand, the power of the government on the property of the citizen, and with the other to bestow it upon favored individuals to aid private enterprises and build up private fortunes, is none the less a robbery because it is done under the forms of law and is called taxation.

Mr. Justice Clifford, on behalf of the self-restraint school of thought, objected that the Court ought not to hold state statutes void without relying on the Constitution or any clause thereof, saying (page 669):

> Such a power is denied to the courts, because to concede it would be to make the courts sovereign over both the Constitution and the people, and convert the government into a judicial despotism.

The next generation of Justices discovered the intricate beauties of the due process clause and used it with telling effect in a long line of cases in which they were sure that they knew what was good for the country. Their zeal in protecting the people from the mistakes of their elected representatives was described by Mr. Justice Holmes, dissenting in *Baldwin v. Missouri,* 281 U. S. 586 (1930), as " . . . evoking a constitutional prohibition from the void of 'due process of law'. . . ."

Speaking of the constitutional rights of the states, he said (page 595):

> As the decisions now stand, I see hardly any limit but the sky to the invalidating of those rights if they happen to strike a majority of this court as for any reason undesirable. I cannot believe that the Amendment was intended to give us carte blanche to embody

our economic or moral beliefs in its prohibitions.

But every man has his breaking point, and Holmes himself was faced with a temptation to do good that he could not resist. He was sceptical of many things, but not of the fundamental importance of freedom of speech. It took a long while for the Justices to get around to the notion that they could force freedom of speech on the states. As late as 1922, Mr. Justice Holmes joined in the opinion in *Prudential Insurance Company v. Cheek,* 259 U. S. 530, which said (page 543):

> . . . neither the 14th Amendment nor any other provision of the Constitution of the United States imposes upon the states any restrictions about "freedom of speech". . . .

Three years later it turned out that his brethren were ready, able and willing to bring freedom of speech under the aegis of due process of law. For twenty years Holmes had been fighting a rear-guard action against the extension of the due process clause. He would have had to be more than human to resist this particular extension and he did not resist it. He was 84 years old. In *Gitlow v. New York,* 268 U. S. 652, in a dissenting opinion, he said:

> The general principle of free speech, it seems to me, must be taken to be included in the Fourteenth Amendment, in view of the scope that has been given to the word "liberty" as there used. . . .

The most articulate champion of the doctrine of self-restraint on the Bench today is Mr. Justice Black. He implores his colleagues to give up their natural law doctrines and go back to a study of the text of the document and the history from which it grew. Dissenting in *Adamson v. California,* 332 U. S. 46 (1947), he said:

> This decision reasserts a constitutional theory spelled out in *Twining v. New Jersey,* 211 U. S. 78, 53 L. ed. 97, 29 S. Ct. 14, that this Court is endowed by the Constitution with boundless power under "natural laws" periodically to expand and contract constitutional standards to conform to the Court's conception of what at a particular time constitutes "civilized decency" and "fundamental liberty and justice."
>
> * * *
>
> I think that decision and the "natural law" theory of the Constitution upon which it relies degrade the constitutional safeguards of the Bill of Rights and simultaneously appropriate for this Court a broad power which we are not authorized by the Constitution to exercise.
>
> * * *
>
> And I further contend that the "natural law" formula which the Court uses to reach its conclusion in this case should be abandoned as an incongruous excrescence on our Constitution. I believe that formula to be itself a violation of our Constitution, in that it subtly conveys to courts, at the expense of legislatures, ultimate power over public policies in fields where no specific provision of the Constitution limits legislative power.
>
> * * *
>
> But this formula also has been used in the past, and can be used in the future, to license this Court, in considering regulatory legislation, to roam at large in the broad expanses of policy and morals and to trespass, all too freely, on the legislative domain of the States as well as the Federal Government.

In *Brown v. Board of Education,* 347 U. S. 483, the Court forbade the states to maintain segregated public schools. In *Bolling v. Sharpe,* 347 U. S. 497, the Court forbade the Congress of the United States to maintain segregated public schools. Both cases were decided the same day, May 17, 1954.

In the *Brown Case* (dealing with state schools) the Court called for the facts of history (as Mr. Justice Black did in *Adamson*). After thousands of hours of laborious research the facts of history were produced: they proved that nobody in 1868 expected the Fourteenth Amendment to abolish segregation. (See Alexander M. Bickel: *The Original Understanding and the Segregation Decision*, 69 Harv. L. Rev. 1.) The facts of history were dismissed as irrelevant and immaterial. The Court knocked out state segregation on the basis of the equal protection clause, saying:

> This disposition makes unnecessary any discussion whether such segregation also violates the Due Process Clause of the Fourteenth Amendment.

But in *Bolling* the Court abolished segregation solely on the basis of the due process clause, thereby demonstrating that it would have reached the same result in *Brown* if the equal protection clause had never been adopted.

In the *Bolling Case* the Court did not call for research into the facts of history. In 1791, nobody thought that the Bill of Rights abolished even slavery, but the Court held in 1954 that words not intended to abolish slavery were intended to abolish segregation.

The basis for the decision in the *Bolling Case* is stated by the Court at the end of its opinion (page 500):

> In view of our decision that the Constitution prohibits the states from maintaining racially segregated public schools, it would be unthinkable that the same Constitution would impose a lesser duty on the Federal Government.

This *non sequitur* is unique. The clause of the Constitution on which the state decision is exclusively based does not impose *any* duty on the Federal Government, as the Court pointed out on the previous page of its opinion (page 499):

> The Fifth Amendment, which is applicable in the District of Columbia, does not contain an equal protection clause as does the Fourteenth Amendment which applies only to the states.

A lawyer would be laughed out of court who argued with a straight face:

> In view of your decision that the constitution prohibits the states from impairing the obligation of contracts, it would be unthinkable that the same constitution would impose a lesser duty on the Federal Government.

When you say that something is "unthinkable" you are expressing as forcefully as you can the strength of your convictions. You mean that no honest and rational person could disagree with you. The Court does not say that segregation is unthinkable. The unthinkable thing is "that the same Constitution would impose a lesser duty on the Federal Government." The argument runs that if the Constitution forbids the states to do some evil thing, it is unthinkable that it would impose a lesser duty on the Federal Government. Heretofore the rule of decision has turned on whether the Constitution does forbid something, rather than on whether it would forbid something. What the Court calls unthinkable is that the Constitution "would" forbid an evil in the states and not in the District. Between September 17, 1787, and May 17, 1954, the doctrine the Court calls unthinkable had been universally thought.

The Court could have avoided this difficulty, and could have got out of the frying pan into the fire, by deciding the federal school case first or by basing the state school cases on the due process clause.

The 1791 Amendment says: "No person shall be . . . deprived of life, liberty, or property, without due process of law. . . ."

The 1868 Amendment says: ". . . nor shall any State deprive any person of life, liberty, or property, without due process of law. . . ."

Thus the Amendment applicable only to the United States and the Amendment applicable only to the states both contain the same words; and, if the Court had first forbidden segregation in the District on the basis of those words, it would have followed logically that the same words would necessarily produce the same result in the states. The Court passed up the chance to hold that exactly the same words mean exactly the same thing, in favor of holding that widely different words produce exactly the same result. The Court decided the state case first and then held that the state case governed the federal case. That would have followed if the decision in the state case had been based on the due process clause; but the Court did not use the due process clause in the state case even as a makeweight.

If the Court had decided the federal case first, the expensive and useless research into the history of the equal protection clause would not have occurred and there would have been no debate over the facts of history. For 165 years any colored children who were educated in the nation's capital were educated in separate schools. The Justices knew that it would sound silly to ask counsel to search for evidence that the framers of the Fifth Amendment intended it to abolish segregation.

But if the Court had begun at the beginning, it would have had to begin with a clause of the Constitution adopted in 1791 that did not keep the Congress from passing and the courts from upholding the Fugitive Slave Law of 1850. Members of Congress and Presidents of the United States also swear to support the Constitution; and they had not thought it necessary to integrate the schools in the District of Columbia. The psychological treatises cited by the Court would have justified Congress in abolishing segregation in the District, because for many years it has been well understood that the police power is the power to adopt and enforce a policy to prevent an evil, and that the writings of experts can be cited in support of the argument that what the legislature seeks to forbid could be thought to be an evil. And if the Court had cited the learned treatises in support of its decision based on the due process clause, it would have sounded as if the Court was citing them to support its own exercise of the police power.

The Court does not say in so many words that it adheres to the dogmas of "natural law," but these school cases are not the first in which natural law considerations have played a decisive part. They give comfort to those who believe that the eternal verities should take precedence over the written law, and they are disturbing to those who prefer a written constitution. Progressive modification by the judges of the judge-made common law is a very different thing from abruptly changing a written constitution. If the eternal verities as revealed through the writings of Gunnar Myrdal are to outweigh the words written in the constitution, the concept of the constitution as a solemn and binding contract is destroyed.

The meaning of judicial self-restraint is that the judge will successfully restrain himself from putting his own convictions ahead of the law. If he does not like the written Constitution, it is not for him, in the words of Omar, to "shatter it to bits — and then re-mould it nearer to the Heart's Desire," or, in the no less eloquent words of Mr. Justice Black, "to roam at large in the broad expanses of policy and morals and to trespass, all too freely, on the legislative domain of the states as well as the Federal Government."

But, as Mr. Justice Black has said, the Court has for many years been roaming at large in the broad expanses of policy and morals; and, as Mr. Justice Holmes intimated, the Court has often embodied its own economic and moral beliefs in the due process clause; and, as Mr. Justice Clifford pointed out eighty years ago, that sort of thing leads to judicial despotism. The strongest denunciations of the Supreme Court are found, not in the speeches of soapbox orators, but in the opinions of dissenting Justices.

In past cases in which the Court has injected its moral views into the picture, it has not upset the domestic institutions of the states. When the Court was holding in a long line of cases, subsequently overruled, that intangible property taxed by one state cannot be taxed by another, there was no concerted outcry from the supporters of a written constitution: the decisions pleased more people than they annoyed. The same thing can be said of the Court's holdings in the realm of freedom of speech and freedom of religion. Most people agree that there is a moral foundation for those decisions; although the constitutional foundation is somewhat shaky. Chief Justice Taney's opinion in the *Dred Scott Case* that an Act of Congress freeing the slaves in the Nebraska Territory deprived the slave owners of their property without due process of law caused a good deal of controversy, but did not interfere with the internal affairs of the states. The school case decisions differ not only in degree but in kind from past examples of "judicial despotism." It is the difference between advancing into forbidden territory step by step and advancing by leaps and bounds. The leaps and bounds began with *Shelly v. Kraemer*, 334 U. S. 1 in 1948. When Chief Justice Vinson wrote the Court's opinion in that case he did not realize what a leap the Court was taking. He found out in *Barrows v. Jackson*, 346 U. S. 249 (1953). In that case, dissenting all by himself, he sputtered (page 267) that the majority opinion:

> puts personal predisposition in a paramount position over well-established proscriptions on power.

He, too, cast a backward glance at the good old days of judicial self-restraint, saying (page 269):

> Since we must rest our decision on the Constitution alone, we must set aside predilections on social policy and adhere to the settled rules which restrict the exercise of our power to judicial review — remembering that the only restraint upon this power is our own sense of self-restraint.

The alarming significance of the school cases extends beyond the immediate decisions. Never before have the personal predilections and moral certainties of the Justices ridden so rough-shod over the text of the written Constitution. The Court has found that the moral law which impels it to advance the interests of colored people outweighs the moral law which teaches that a judge who has sworn to uphold a constitution ought to uphold it. Actually, the Court was not faced with a moral dilemma. A judge is not blameworthy who enforces a written law that he disagrees with, and as a last resort he can resign if the law he has sworn to enforce is more immoral than he can stomach. But the Justices, in the school cases, have trapped in a genuine moral dilemma all those who believe (1) that the Constitution is a binding contract, and (2) that the Supreme Court is the final umpire to interpret that contract.

To illustrate this moral dilemma with a homely example, let us suppose that two teams are tied in the last inning of the World Series and that the umpire is morally convinced that the Yankees ought to win. The Yankee runner is tagged with the ball forty-five feet from the home plate, and the umpire, acting on his understanding of the precepts of natural law, declares that the runner is safe at home. Those who bet on the Dodgers are then confronted with the problem of whether the moral law requires them to pay their bets, and those who bet on the Yankees are confronted with the problem of whether the moral law permits them to accept the payments. Does the decision of the umpire prevail over the rules of the game? One of the rules of the game is that both teams shall obey the decision of the umpire; and the umpire has promised to stick to the rule book.

The price of judicial independence is that the people are dependent on judicial self-restraint. The people have made this bargain on the understanding that the judges will render equal justice under law and will not enforce their personal convictions in lieu of law. Those who understand what the court has done can hardly think it immoral to protest and to resist. It has been suggested in support of what the Court has done that "world opinion" is pleased by the result. No worse reason could be suggested. No decision of a court is going to stem the torrent of Communist propaganda, and even if it did, the preservation of the Constitution is more important than the approval of the Kremlin. Even those who are most sensitive to world opinion have not recommended that amendments to our constitution should be made by a vote of three fourths of the members of the General Assembly of the United Nations.

The school decisions have raised acrimonious issues between North and South and within the political parties, and those issues, by exciting specific and dramatic controversies, have obscured the one great issue: whether the people of this country really believe that any immediate reform can possibly be worth more to the United States than the preservation of the Constitution of the United States.

III. SEGREGATION: THE REACTION

Robert A. Leflar and *Wylie H. Davis*: DEVICES TO EVADE OR DELAY DESEGREGATION

SINCE segregation in the schools [is] unlawful, the effort to eliminate it as a fact will probably be more affected by the defensive procedures and frustrative or dilatory devices employed than by the affirmative legal remedies used to further the effort. Some of these defensive weapons will be purely factual and will turn upon finances, jobs, personal pressures, and other similar economic and social considerations, which are sometimes embodied in the form of law and sometimes not. Some will be legislative. Many will be administrative, designed perhaps to give a front of legality to contrary facts that may or may not be effectively concealed by carefully kept records in a superintendent's office. In other instances skilled lawyers will exploit the techniques of a system of law which from its beginnings has often made it easier to delay relief than to give it, particularly when judges honestly sympathize with defendants' views. Much of the compliance litigation, if school segregation should be held unconstitutional, will be framed by such tactics of resistance.

A. Financial Non-Support

A state strongly opposed to mixed schools might use its power over allocation of state funds so as to prevent local school districts from complying, or fully complying, with desegregation requirements. By conditioning allotments upon the maintenance of segregation, a state might induce districts, otherwise willing to desegregate, to delay the change until the last possible moment. . . . Even after superior law actually forces desegregation upon a district, or upon all districts in a state, the withdrawal of state aid might not end, and could thus directly affect the quality of the desegregated schools and thereby indirectly affect the desegregation program itself. Deliberate under-financing of desegregated schools, either through withdrawal of state appropriations or through decreased tax support in individual districts, will result in poorer schools. Under such circumstances most well-to-do families would presumably send their children to segregated private schools, and the desegregated public schools would become badly financed institutions attended mostly by Negroes and poor whites. The latter combination would, however, once their interests clearly coincided, be more potent politically than the prosperous white families, and eventually there might be such popular demand for improvement of the common schools that district and state support would be reestablished and the schools would improve anew.

B. Abandonment of Education as a State Function

. . . It is possible that some of the

From the *Harvard Law Review*, Vol. 67, January, 1954, No. 3, pp. 377–429. Reprinted by permission.

Southern states will attempt to evade the new requirements by divorcing their school systems from the machinery of government as such. South Carolina has already gone a long way toward amending its constitution to that effect, and some other states have taken preliminary steps. The thinking behind these proposals is that the schools might be operated in the future by private groups or organizations not bound by the Fourteenth Amendment.

* * *

If a state transfers all its public school facilities to private groups like churches, civil or fraternal societies, newly organized benevolent corporations, or school "cooperatives" created for the purpose, then there will almost surely have to be either direct financing of such groups from tax revenues or indirect state assistance in collecting fees and assessments or otherwise establishing a fairly stable financial and attendance structure for the new educational bodies. . . .

This, however, would almost inevitably result in eventual characterization of the overall operation as state action. . . .

On the other hand, it must be recognized that, though the ultimate legal consequence of turning the public schools over to so-called private agencies for segregated operation would very probably mean a United States Supreme Court determination of unconstitutionality, it would take the courts some time to arrive at that finale, particularly through piecemeal litigation. It can be anticipated that the states, school districts, and private agencies affected would fight the cases vigorously at all stages. They might change their "private" school substitutes from one form to another after the first was invalidated, then litigate anew on the chameleonized facts. They might start out with direct state subsidies of privately operated schools, and hope that by the time this system was condemned they would be prepared to shift, with some prospect of successful operation, to a contrivance having a less direct nexus with the state. A good many years of delay in desegregation could in any event be achieved by these tactics, and in the meantime educational possibilities more realistic than those which are abstractly predictable might conceivably be worked out in practice.

C. Superficial Compliances

It may be anticipated that many and in some states all school districts will, . . . undertake surface compliance only. While asserting conformity, they will at the same time try to keep desegregation to a minimum or perhaps to escape it entirely. A variety of devices looking to this end might be thought serviceable in varying degrees.

Gerrymandering of attendance districts is probably the most obvious of such devices. . . . By establishing schools in each of such sections and tailoring the attendance districts to fit the separate residential areas, local authorities may be able to retain substantial segregation in some communities without formally disobeying desegregation requirements.

* * *

[But] the Negroes' legal right to expand the so-called colored sections and to move into "exclusive" white sections is of course assured by Supreme Court holdings that residential restriction laws and ordinances are invalid, and that even private exclusionary contracts based on race are unenforceable under the Fourteenth Amendment.

If attendance districts are so contoured as to skip houses or blocks or to extend geographical peninsulas and islands into physically unified areas solely for the purpose of including families of a particular race, it is reasonably certain that the districting would be regarded as an invalid evasion of desegregation requirements. On the other hand, a geographically compact and physically reasonable district might well be approved judicially even though it were deliberately planned as all-Negro or all-white. . . .

Another possible form of superficial compliance would involve the continued maintenance of Negro schools for entire communities, regardless of residential areas, with local pressures designed to influence most Negroes to attend them "voluntarily," though qualified Negroes demanding admittance to white schools might be accommodated. No one has seriously contended that the Equal Protection Clause *requires* all Negro children to attend desegregated schools. The rights safeguarded by the clause are personal; an individual presumably can either claim or waive them. Of course, the local pressures exerted to secure Negro attendance at separate schools would be purely private and unofficial. Negro children admitted to white schools, and their parents, might be so treated by other students, neighbors, employers, and fellow citizens generally as to make them personally unhappy, thereby inducing them to withdraw rather than suffer — at the same time deterring others from applying. . . .

Closely related is the possibility that school officials, in a district retaining separate Negro schools, might announce that qualified Negro pupils on application would be admitted to "white" schools in the district, but that certain examinations and other matriculation "routine" would be required of all students, white and colored, applying for such admission. The administrative procedure might then be so complicated that rejected Negro applicants would have difficulty in complying with it, especially if a discriminatory stewardship were well concealed in the bureaucratic webs and meshes of the administrative process.

* * *

The court cannot take over a school committee's duty to give examinations, and racial discrimination in fact would be an uncertain inference unless failing grades given along racial lines could be shown by the district's treatment of a large number of children. Even with reference to a large number, specific instances of discrimination might have to be identified, which could leave the bulk of the unequal treatment still unaffected. Discriminatory administration of other "rational" standards for the admission of all children, such as criteria of morals, physical or mental infirmity, or "filthiness," would be similarly difficult for the courts to uncover in many instances. The administrative stumbling blocks suggested are only a beginning. The number and variety available to school officials and districts are confined more by the limits of personal ingenuity than by judicial restraint.

* * *

D. The Law's Delays

Each school district that fails to comply with desegregation requirements normally represents a separate lawsuit. The volume of litigation necessary to enforce widespread compliance within an unwilling state whose Negro population is widely distributed would be tremendous. True, the class action device, and the possibility of consolidating suits for purposes of trial, would serve somewhat to alleviate the burden, but the time consumed by such litigation would in any event be lengthy, and the expense great.

* * *

The classic illustration of such dilatory

tactics is the *Alton* case in Illinois, in which one Negro plaintiff won each of five appeals to the supreme court of his state over a ten-year period, yet saw his children grow up without ever having been admitted to unsegregated schools in accordance with that state's law. The same sort of intransigent local resistance to enforcement of clear legal rights is at least equally possible in the South today, and the possibility may be increased if jury trials should be involved.

* * *

LEGAL REMEDIES FOR ENFORCING COMPLIANCE WITH DESEGREGATION OR EQUALIZATION REQUIREMENTS

An announcement by the United States Supreme Court as to what the Constitution requires by way of desegregation or equalization of public schools, being immediately binding only on the parties actually before the Court in the decided cases, will still leave much for the courts and the law to do before the announced rule operates effectively in the school districts of America. School officials and districts not yet sued may choose to wait and comply with the law only when they are compelled to do so. . . .

The class suit device can, at least to some extent, alleviate the problem of excessive litigation inherent in this situation. . . . By combining in one suit the claims of all potential plaintiffs in the district, some of "the law's delays" may be avoided.

Occasionally the issue may be effectively settled within a single district by a "taxpayer's suit" to restrain improper expenditures of public funds. . . . A bond buyer might sue to rescind his contract of purchase if the bond proceeds were earmarked for constitutionally doubtful purposes.

* * *

Since the development of the remedy of declaratory judgments in the last few years, Negro plaintiffs in the public school cases have come increasingly to combine prayers for declaratory and injunctive relief. This combination of remedies seems to serve best the points of view of plaintiffs, defendants, and courts in affording a matrix for full analysis and disposition of all the facets of a complex case. Punishment for contempt is normally available as an enforcement sanction in such cases, and the threat of its summary employment by fine or imprisonment is sometimes needed to coerce obedience. . . .

The action for damages for deprivation of valuable constitutional rights has not been much used in the public school segregation and equalization cases. It is apparently available. . . . The right to attend the proper school may be valuable to the individual pupil, and perhaps also to his parents. Although it is a kind of right not easily evaluated in pecuniary terms, some measurement is possible. . . . In public school situations such damage suits would presumably be brought against school principals, superintendents, boards of education, and other officials administering the allegedly unconstitutional program. Substantial money damage claims against recalcitrant school officials might be more effective than most of the other available sanctions, though their effectiveness may be somewhat lessened by the fact that such suits are ordinarily triable before local juries. . . .

A closely related federal remedy imposes a criminal penalty upon any person who under color of state law deprives another, by reason of such other's race or color, of rights secured or protected by the Constitution or laws of the United States. In the past this penalty has not often been invoked in public school cases; but as the rights of Negroes in the education field are clarified, one may expect that it will be oftener suggested.

A JOINT RESOLUTION OF THE STATE OF SOUTH CAROLINA

CONDEMNING And Protesting The Usurpation And Encroachment On The Reserved Powers Of The States By The Supreme Court Of The United States, Calling Upon The States And Congress To Prevent This And Other Encroachment By The Central Government And Declaring The Intention Of South Carolina To Exercise All Powers Reserved To It, To Protect Its Sovereignty And The Rights Of Its People.

Mindful of its responsibilities to its own citizens and of its obligations to the other States, the General Assembly of South Carolina adopts this Resolution in condemnation of and protest against the illegal encroachment by the central government into the reserved powers of the States and the rights of the people, and against the grave threat to constitutional government, implicit in the recent decisions of the Supreme Court of the United States, for these reasons:

1. The genius of the American Constitution lies in two provisions. It establishes a clear division between the powers delegated by the States to the central government and the powers reserved to the States, or to the people. As a prerequisite to any lawful redistribution of these powers, it establishes as a part of the process for its amendment the requirement of approval by the States.

The division of these powers is reaffirmed in the Tenth Amendment to the Constitution in these words: "The powers not delegated to the United States by the Constitution, nor prohibited by it to the States, are reserved to the States respectively, or to the people."

Long judicial precedent also clearly reaffirms that the central government is one of delegated powers, specifically enumerated in the Constitution, and that all other powers of government, not prohibited by the Constitution to the States, are reserved to the States or to the people.

The power to propose changes and the power to approve changes in the basic law is specifically stated by Article V of the Constitution in these words: "The Congress, whenever two thirds of both houses shall deem it necessary, shall propose amendments to this Constitution, or, on the application of the legislatures of two thirds of the several states, shall call a convention for proposing amendments, which, in either case, shall be valid to all intents and purposes, as part of this Constitution, when ratified by the legislatures of three fourths of the several states, or by conventions in three fourths thereof, as the one or the other mode of ratification may be proposed by the Congress. . . ."

Lincoln, in his first inaugural, recognized these constitutional principles in the following language: "The maintenance inviolate to (sic) the rights of the States, and especially the right of each State to order and control its own domestic institutions, according to its own judgment exclusively, is essential to that balance of power on which the perfection and endurance of our political fabric depend. . . ."

2. Neither the judicial power delegated to the Supreme Court in Article III of the Constitution nor such appellate jurisdiction as the Article authorizes the

Congress to confer upon the Court, makes the Court the Supreme Arbiter of the rights of the States under the compact.

3. The right of each of the States to maintain at its own expense racially separate public schools for the children of its citizens and other racially separate public facilities is not forbidden or limited by the language or the intent of the Fourteenth Amendment. This meaning of the Fourteenth Amendment was established beyond reasonable question by the action of the Congress in providing for racially segregated schools in the District of Columbia by legislation contemporaneous with the submission of the Fourteenth Amendment to the States in 1866, and by the fact that a majority of the States in the Union at that time recognized that segregation in public facilities had not been abolished by this Amendment. There is no evidence in the Constitution, in the Amendments, or in any contemporary document that the States intended to give to the central government the right to invade the sanctity of the homes of America and deny to responsible parents a meaningful voice in the training of their children or in the selection of associates for them.

4. For almost sixty years, beginning in 1896, an unbroken line of decisions of the Court interpreted the Fourteenth Amendment as recognizing the right of the States to maintain racially separate public facilities for their people. If the Court in the interpretation of the Constitution is to depart from the sanctity of past decisions and to rely on the current political and social philosophy of its members to unsettle the great constitutional principles so clearly established, the rights of individuals are not secure and government under a written Constitution has no stability.

5. Disregarding the plain language of the Fourteenth Amendment, ignoring the conclusive character of the contemporary actions of the Congress and of the State legislatures, overruling its own decisions to the contrary, the Supreme Court of the United States on May 17, 1954, relying on its own views of sociology and psychology, for the first time held that the Fourteenth Amendment prohibited the States from maintaining racially separate public schools and since then the Court has enlarged this to include other public facilities. In so doing the Court, under the guise of interpretation, amended the Constitution of the United States, thus usurping the power of Congress to submit, and that of the several States to approve, constitutional changes. This action of the Court ignored the principle that the meaning of the Constitution and of its Amendments does not change. It is a written instrument. That which the Fourteenth Amendment meant when adopted it means now (*South Carolina v. United States,* 199 U. S. 437, 449).

6. The educational opportunities of white and colored children in the public schools of South Carolina have been substantially improved during recent years and highly satisfactory results are being obtained in our segregated schools. If enforced, the decision of the Court will seriously impair and retard the education of the children of both races, will nullify these recent advances and will cause untold friction between the races.

7. Tragic as are the consequences of this decision to the education of the children of both races in the Southern States, the usurpation of constitutional power by the Court transcends the problems of segregation in education. The Court holds that regardless of the meaning of a constitutional provision when adopted, and in the language of the 1955 Report of the Gray Commission to the Governor

of Virginia, "irrespective of precedent, long acquiesced in, the Court can and will change its interpretation of the Constitution at its pleasure, disregarding the orderly processes for its Amendment set forth in Article V thereof. It means that the most fundamental of the Rights of the States or of their citizens exist by the Court's sufferance and that the law of the land is whatever the Court may determine it to be. . . ." Thus the Supreme Court, created to preserve the Constitution, has planted the seed for the destruction of constitutional government.

8. Because the preservation of the rights of the States is as much within the design and care of the Constitution as the preservation of the national government, since "the Constitution, in all of its provisions, looks to an indestructible Union, composed of indestructible States" (*Texas v. White* [1869], 7 Wallace 700, 725), and since the usurpation of the rights reserved to the States is by the judicial branch of the central government, the issues raised by this decision are of such grave import as to require this sovereign State to judge for itself of the infraction of the Constitution.

Be it enacted by the General Assembly of the State of South Carolina:

SECTION 1. That the States have never delegated to the central government the power to change the Constitution nor have they surrendered to the central government the power to prohibit to the States the right to maintain racially separate but equal public facilities or the right to determine when such facilities are in the best interest of their citizens.

SECTION 2. That the action of the Supreme Court of the United States constitutes a deliberate, palpable, and dangerous attempt to change the true intent and meaning of the Constitution. It is in derogation of the power of Congress to propose, and that of the States to approve, constitutional changes. It thereby establishes a judicial precedent, if allowed to stand, for the ultimate destruction of constitutional government.

SECTION 3. That the State of South Carolina condemns and protests against the illegal encroachment by the central government into the reserved powers of the States and the rights of the people and against the grave threat to the constitutional government implicit in the decisions of the Supreme Court of the United States.

SECTION 4. That the States and the Congress do take appropriate legal steps to prevent, now and in the future, usurpation of power by the Supreme Court and other encroachment by the central government into the reserved powers of the States and the rights of the people to the end that our American system of Constitutional government may be preserved.

SECTION 5. In the meantime, the State of South Carolina as a loyal and sovereign State of the Union will exercise the powers reserved to it under the Constitution to judge for itself of the infractions and to take such other legal measures as it may deem appropriate to protect its sovereignty and the rights of its people.

SECTION 6. That a copy of this Resolution be sent to the Governor and Legislature of each of the other States, to the President of the United States, to each of the Houses of Congress, to South Carolina's Representatives and Senators in the Congress, and to the Supreme Court of the United States for its information.

SECTION 7. This act shall take effect upon its approval by the Governor.
In the Senate House the 14th day of February
In the Year of Our Lord One Thousand Nine Hundred and Fifty-six.

ERNEST F. HOLLINGS,
President of the Senate

SOLOMON BLATT,
Speaker of the House of Representatives

Approved the 14th day of February, 1956.
GEORGE BELL TIMMERMAN, JR.,
Governor

Senator Sam J. Ervin, Jr.: DECLARATION OF CONSTITUTIONAL PRINCIPLES

THE unwarranted decision of the Supreme Court in the public school cases is now bearing the fruit always produced when men substitute naked power for established law.

The Founding Fathers gave us a Constitution of checks and balances because they realized the inescapable lesson of history that no man or group of men can be safely entrusted with unlimited power. They framed this Constitution with its provisions for change by amendment in order to secure the fundamentals of government against the dangers of temporary popular passion or the personal predilections of public office holders.

We regard the decision of the Supreme Court in the school cases as a clear abuse of judicial power. It climaxes a trend in the Federal Judiciary undertaking to legislate, in derogation of the authority of Congress, and to encroach upon the reserved rights of the States and the people.

The original Constitution does not mention education. Neither does the Fourteenth Amendment nor any other Amendment. The debates preceding the submission of the Fourteenth Amendment clearly show that there was no intent that it should affect the systems of education maintained by the States.

The very Congress which proposed the Amendment subsequently provided for segregated schools in the District of Columbia.

When the Amendment was adopted in 1868, there were 37 States of the Union. Every one of the 26 States that had any substantial racial differences among its people either approved the operation of segregated schools already in existence or subsequently established such schools by action of the same law-making body which considered the Fourteenth Amendment.

As admitted by the Supreme Court in the public school case (*Brown v. Board of Education*), the doctrine of separate but equal schools "apparently originated in *Roberts v. City of Boston* . . . (1849), upholding school segregation against attack as being violative of a State constitutional guarantee of equality." This constitutional doctrine began in the North — not in the South, and it was followed not only in Massachusetts, but in Connecticut, New York, Illinois, Indiana, Michigan, Minnesota, New Jersey, Ohio, Pennsylvania and other northern States until

Statement by U.S. Senator Sam J. Ervin, Jr., of North Carolina, signed by seventeen Senators and seventy-seven Representatives, and presented in both Houses March 12, 1956.

they, exercising their rights as States through the constitutional processes of local self-government, changed their school systems.

In the case of *Plessy v. Ferguson* in 1896 the Supreme Court expressly declared that under the Fourteenth Amendment no person was denied any of his rights if the States provided separate but equal public facilities. This decision has been followed in many other cases. It is notable that the Supreme Court, speaking through Chief Justice Taft, a former President of the United States, unanimously declared in 1927 in *Lum v. Rice* that the "separate but equal" principle is ". . . within the discretion of the State in regulating its public schools and does not conflict with the Fourteenth Amendment."

This interpretation, restated time and again, became a part of the life of the people of many of the States and confirmed their habits, customs, traditions and way of life. It is founded on elemental humanity and common sense, for parents should not be deprived by government of the right to direct the lives and education of their own children.

Though there has been no constitutional amendment or Act of Congress changing this established legal principle almost a century old, the Supreme Court of the United States, with no legal basis for such action, undertook to exercise their naked judicial power and substituted their personal political and social ideas for the established law of the land.

This unwarranted exercise of power by the Court, contrary to the Constitution, is creating chaos and confusion in the States principally affected. It is destroying the amicable relations between the white and Negro races that have been created through 90 years of patient effort by the good people of both races. It has planted hatred and suspicion where there has been heretofore friendship and understanding.

Without regard to the consent of the governed, outside agitators are threatening immediate and revolutionary changes in our public school systems. If done, this is certain to destroy the system of public education in some of the States.

With the gravest concern for the explosive and dangerous condition created by this decision and inflamed by outside meddlers:

We reaffirm our reliance on the Constitution as the fundamental law of the land.

We decry the Supreme Court's encroachments on rights reserved to the States and to the people, contrary to established law and to the Constitution.

We commend the motives of those States which have declared the intention to resist forced integration by any lawful means.

We appeal to the States and people who are not directly affected by these decisions to consider the constitutional principles involved against the time when they too, on issues vital to them, may be the victims of judicial encroachment.

Even though we constitute a minority in the present Congress, we have full faith that a majority of the American people believe in the dual system of government which has enabled us to achieve our greatness and will in time demand that the reserved rights of the States and of the people be made secure against judicial usurpation.

We pledge ourselves to use all lawful means to bring about a reversal of this decision which is contrary to the Constitution and to prevent the use of force in its implementation.

In this trying period, as we all seek to right this wrong, we appeal to our people not to be provoked by the agitators and troublemakers invading our States and to scrupulously refrain from disorder and lawless acts.

Senator Sam J. Ervin, Jr.: ALEXANDER HAMILTON'S PHANTOM

IF I am to talk to you about what is happening to the law of the land and the sovereignty of the States, I must discuss with candor how and why the Supreme Court of the United States is usurping and exercising powers which the Constitution of the United States vests in the Congress or reserves to the States.

I know it is not popular in some quarters to tell the truth about the Supreme Court. Admonitions of this character come to us daily from such quarters: "When the Supreme Court speaks, its decisions must be accepted as sacrosanct by the Bench, the Bar, and the People of America, even though they constitute encroachments on the constitutional domain of the Congress, or reduce the States to meaningless zeros on the nation's map. Indeed, the Bench, the Bar, and the People must do more than this. They must speak of the Supreme Court at all times with a reverence akin to that which inspired Job to speak thus of Jehovah: 'Though He slay me, yet will I trust Him.'"

Such admonitions are intellectual rubbish. Americans are not required to believe in the infallibility of judges. They have an inalienable right to think and speak their honest thoughts concerning decisions of Supreme Court majorities and all other things under the sun. When all is said, a public officer receives the confidence and respect he merits, no more and no less, whether he be President, Senator, Judge, or Dogcatcher. This is as it should be. The Supreme Court will justly forfeit all claim to the confidence and respect of the Bench, the Bar, and the citizens of our country if it flouts George Washington's warning that usurpation "is the customary weapon by which free governments are destroyed" and refuses to confine its activities to its own constitutional sphere.

My endeavor to tell the truth about the Supreme Court must begin with the Constitutional Convention of 1787.

The men who composed the American Constitutional Convention of 1787 comprehended in full measure the everlasting political truth that no man or set of men can be safely trusted with governmental power of an unlimited nature. In consequence, they were determined, above all things, to establish a government of laws and not of men.

To prevent the exercise of arbitrary power by the Federal Government, they inserted in the Constitution of the United States the doctrine of the separation of governmental powers. In so doing, they utilized the doctrine of the separation of powers in a twofold way. They delegated to the Federal Government the powers necessary to enable it to discharge its limited functions as a central government, and they left to each state the power to regulate its own internal affairs. It was this use of the doctrine of the separation of powers which prompted Chief Justice Salmon P. Chase to make

From an address by Senator Sam J. Ervin, Jr. (D-NC) to the State Bar of Texas at Houston, Texas, on July 7, 1956.

these memorable remarks in his opinion in *Texas v. White:*

> Not only, therefore, can there be no loss of separate and independent autonomy to the States, through their union under the Constitution, but it may be not unreasonably said that the preservation of the States, and the maintenance of their governments, are as much within the design and care of the Constitution as the preservation of the Union and the maintenance of the National Government. THE CONSTITUTION, IN ALL ITS PROVISIONS, LOOKS TO AN INDISSOLUBLE UNION, COMPOSED OF INDESTRUCTIBLE STATES.

In their other utilization of the doctrine of the separation of powers, the members of the Convention of 1787 vested the power to make laws in the Congress, the power to execute laws in the President, and the power to interpret laws in the Supreme Court of the United States and such inferior courts as the Congress might establish. Moreover, they declared, in essence, that the legislative, the executive, and the judicial powers of the Federal Government should forever remain separate and distinct from each other.

The members of the Convention of 1787 did not put their sole reliance upon the doctrine of the separation of governmental powers in their effort to forestall the exercise of arbitrary power by the Federal Government. They balanced the President's power to veto the acts of Congress against the powers of Congress to legislate, and they balanced the power of Congress over the purse against the President's power as Commander in Chief of the Army and Navy. They made the Supreme Court of the United States independent of the President and the Congress by giving its judges life tenure during good behavior and by providing that their compensation should not be diminished during their continuance in office. They failed, however, to place in the Constitution any provisions to restrain any abuse of its judicial power by the Supreme Court of the United States.

This significant omission was not overlooked at the time. Elbridge Gerry, a delegate from Massachusetts, asserted:

> There are no well defined limits of the Judiciary Powers, they seem to be left as a boundless ocean, that has broken over the chart of the Supreme Lawgiver, *thus far shalt thou go and no further,* and as they cannot be comprehended by the clearest capacity, or the most sagacious mind, it would be an Herculean labour to attempt to describe the dangers with which they are replete.

George Mason, a delegate from Virginia, made this more specific objection:

> The judiciary of the United States is so constructed and extended as to absorb and destroy the judiciaries of the several states. . . .

Others declared, in substance, that under the Constitution the decisions of the Supreme Court of the United States would "not be in any manner subject to . . . revision or correction"; that "the power of construing the laws" would enable the Supreme Court of the United States "to mould them into whatever shape it" should "think proper"; that the Supreme Court of the United States could "substitute" its "own pleasure" for the law of the land; and that the "errors and usurpations of the Supreme Court of the United States" would "be uncontrollable and remediless."

Alexander Hamilton rejected these arguments with this emphatic assertion: "The supposed danger of Judiciary encroachments . . . is, in reality, a phantom." He declared, in essence, that this assertion was true because men selected to sit on the Supreme Court of the United States would "be chosen with a view to those qualifications which fit men for the stations of Judges," and that they would give "that inflexible and uniform adherence" to legal rules "which we perceive to be indispensable in the courts of justice."

In elaborating this thesis, Alexander Hamilton said: "It has been frequently remarked with great propriety, that a voluminous code of laws is one of the inconveniences necessarily connected with the advantages of a free government. To avoid an arbitrary discretion in the courts, it is indispensable that they should be bound down by strict rules and precedents, which serve to define and point out their duty in every particular case that comes before them; and it will readily be conceived, from the variety of controversies which grow out of the folly and wickedness of mankind, that the records of those precedents must unavoidably swell to a very considerable bulk, and must demand long and laborious study to acquire a competent knowledge of them. Hence, it is that there can be but few men in . . . society, who will have sufficient skills in the laws to qualify them for the station of Judges."

By these remarks, Hamilton assured the several States that men selected to sit upon the Supreme Court of the United States would be able and willing to subject themselves to the restraint inherent in the judicial process. Experience makes this proposition indisputable: Although one may possess a brilliant intellect and be actuated by lofty motives, he is not qualified for the station of a judge in a government of laws unless he is able and willing to subject himself to the restraint inherent in the judicial process.

What is the restraint inherent in the judicial process? The answer to this query appears in the statements of Hamilton. The restraint inherent in the judicial process is the mental discipline which prompts a qualified occupant of a judicial office to lay aside his personal notion of what the law ought to be, and to base his decision on established legal precedents and rules.

How is this mental discipline acquired? The answer to this question likewise appears in the statements of Hamilton. This mental discipline is ordinarily the product of long and laborious legal work as a practicing lawyer, or long and laborious judicial work as a judge of an appellate court or a trial court of general jurisdiction. It is sometimes the product of long and laborious work as a teacher of law. It cannot be acquired by the occupancy of an executive or legislative office. And, unhappily, it can hardly be acquired by those who come or return to the law in late life after spending most of their mature years in other fields of endeavor.

The reasons why the mental discipline required to qualify one for a judicial office is ordinarily the product of long and laborious work as a practicing lawyer, or as an appellate judge, or as a judge of a court of general jurisdiction are rather obvious. Practicing lawyers and judges of courts of general jurisdiction perform their functions in the workaday world where men and women live, move and have their being. To them, law is destitute of social value unless it has sufficient stability to afford reliable rules to govern the conduct of people, and unless it can be found with reasonable certainty in established legal precedents. An additional consideration implants respect for established legal precedents in the minds of judges other than those who sit upon the Supreme Court of the United

States. These judges are accustomed to have their decisions reviewed by higher courts and are certain to be reminded by reversals that they are subject to what Chief Justice Bleckley of the Supreme Court of Georgia called "the fallibility which is inherent in all courts except those of last resort," if they attempt to substitute their personal notions of what they think the law ought to be for the law as it is laid down in established legal precedents.

The States accepted as valid Alexander Hamilton's positive assurance that men chosen to serve on the Supreme Court of the United States would subject themselves to the restraint inherent in the Judicial process, and were thereby induced to ratify the Constitution notwithstanding the omission from that instrument of any express provision protecting the other branches of the Federal Government, the States, or the people against the arbitrary exercise of its judicial power by the Supreme Court.

For several generations next succeeding its utterance, the people of America had no reason to doubt the accuracy of Alexander Hamilton's assurance. With rare exceptions, the Presidents selected for membership upon the Supreme Court of the United States men who had long and laboriously participated in the administration of justice either as practicing lawyers or as judges of State Courts or as judges of the Federal Courts inferior to the Supreme Court. As a consequence, the overwhelming majority of the men called to service upon the Supreme Court were able and willing to subject themselves to the restraint inherent in the judicial process and to perform their tasks in the light of the principle that it is the duty of the judge to interpret the law, not to make it.

* * *

I regret to say, however, that the course of the Supreme Court of the United States in recent years has been such as to cause me to ponder the question whether fidelity to fact ought not to compel us to remove from the portal of the building which houses it the majestic words, "Equal Justice Under Law," and to substitute for them the superscription, "Not justice under law, but justice according to the personal notions of the temporary occupants of this building."...

Candor compels the confession that on many occasions during recent years the Supreme Court has to all intents and purposes usurped the power of the Congress and the States to amend the Constitution. This abuse of power was made manifest even before the decision in *Brown v. Board of Education,* which repudiates solely upon the basis of psychology and sociology the interpretation placed upon the Fourteenth Amendment in respect to racial segregation by Federal and State Courts, the Congress itself, and the Executive branches of the Federal and State Governments throughout the preceding 86 years. . . .

Recent decisions make it manfest that the Supreme Court has usurped the power of Congress to legislate. Perhaps the most glaring of these decisions is *Girouard v. United States,* where the Court overruled three previous decisions and a subsequent confirming act of Congress simply because a majority of its members did not believe that Congress had exercised its legislative power wisely in denying the privilege of citizenship to aliens who were unwilling to bear arms in defense of this country. To be sure, the majority of the Court did not say that it thought that Congress had legislated unwisely. But a statement to this effect would have been a far better reason for its decision than any of those it gave.

In addition to its revolutionary decisions on constitutional and statutory subjects, the Supreme Court of the United States has substantially impaired the doctrine of *stare decisis* and the stability of the law of the land which this doctrine formerly insured by overruling, repudiating, or ignoring its established precedents of earlier years. Former Justice Owen J. Roberts, a recent member of the Court, made this comment in this connection in his dissenting opinion in *Smith v. Allwright:* "The reason for my concern is that the instant decision, overruling that announced about 9 years ago, tends to bring adjudications of this Tribunal into the same class as a restricted railroad ticket, good for this day and train only."

* * *

The question naturally arises: Why does the Supreme Court of the United States prefer to make constitutions and laws rather than to interpret them?

The answer to this question appears in the assurance which Alexander Hamilton gave to the States when he was urging them to ratify the Constitution. It is simply this: The majority of the members of the Supreme Court during recent years have been either unable or unwilling to subject themselves to the restraint inherent in the judicial process.

When all is said, it is not surprising that this is so. The custom of past generations of appointing to membership upon the Supreme Court men who had worked long and laboriously in the administration of justice either as practicing lawyers or as State Judges, or as Judges of Federal Courts inferior to the Supreme Court, has been more honored of late in its breach than in its observance.

All of the members of the Supreme Court are genial gentlemen of high attainments and significant accomplishments. But the majority of them have not worked either long or laboriously as practicing lawyers, or as State Judges or as Judges of the Federal Courts inferior to the Supreme Court. As a consequence, the majority of them have not undergone the mental discipline which enables a qualified occupant of a judicial office to lay aside his personal notions of what the law ought to be and to base his decisions on what the law has been declared to be in legal precedents.

* * *

These facts are astounding:

1. No member of the Supreme Court as it is now constituted, ever served as a judge of a court of general jurisdiction, either State or Federal.

2. No member of the Supreme Court as it is now constituted, ever served as a judge upon an appellate court in any one of the forty-eight states.

3. Only two of the nine members of the Supreme Court, as it is now constituted, ever served as appellate judges on Federal courts inferior to the Supreme Court before they were elevated to their present offices. The combined prior service of these two members totaled only about nine years. Moreover, a majority of the members of the Supreme Court, as it is now constituted, did not devote their major efforts to the actual practice of law before their appointments to the bench.

It is high time for the Bench and the Bar and the People of America to ponder the question whether the country ought not to take action by constitutional amendment or otherwise to make it certain that in the future men will be selected for service upon the Supreme Court because of their possession of what Alexander Hamilton called "those qualifications which fit men for the station of judges," and because of their ability and willingness to subject themselves to the restraint inherent in the judicial process.

It may be that in making these observations, I am merely enacting the role of a fool who rushes in where discreet angels fear to tread. If so, I can plead in extenuation of my folly that I love the American Constitution and know that an indissoluble Union composed of indestructible States cannot endure if our government of laws is destroyed by judicial usurpation.

Senator Hawes: A MEMORIAL TO CONGRESS TO DECLARE THE 14TH AND 15TH AMENDMENTS NULL AND VOID

WHEREAS, the State of Georgia together with the ten other Southern States declared to have been lately in rebellion against the United States, following the termination of hostilities in 1865, met all the conditions laid down by the President of the United States, in the exercise of his Constitutional powers to recognize the governments of states, domestic as well as foreign, for the resumption of practical relations with the Government of the United States, and at the direction of the President did elect Senators and Representatives to the 39th Congress of the United States, as a State and States in proper Constitutional relation to the United States; and

WHEREAS, when the duly elected Senators and Representatives appeared in the Capitol of the United States to take their seats at the time for the opening of the 39th Congress, and again at the times for the openings of the 40th and the 41st Congresses, hostile majorities in both Houses refused to admit them to their seats in manifest violation of Articles I and V of the United States Constitution; and

WHEREAS, the said Congresses, not being constituted of Senators and Representatives from each State as required by the Supreme Law of the Land, were not, in Constitutional contemplation, anything more than private assemblages unlawfully attempting to exercise the Legislative Power of the United States; and

WHEREAS, the so-called 39th Congress, which proposed to the Legislatures of the several States an amendment to the Constitution of the United States, known as the 14th Amendment, and the so-called 40th Congress, which proposed an amendment known as the 15th Amendment, were without lawful power to propose any amendment whatsoever to the Constitution; and

WHEREAS, two-thirds of the Members of the House of Representatives and of the Senate, as they should have been constituted, failed to vote for the submission of these amendments, and,

WHEREAS, All proceedings subsequently flowing from these invalid proposals, purporting to establish the so-called 14th and 15th Amendments as valid parts of the Constitution, were null and void and of no effect from the beginning, and

WHEREAS, furthermore, when these invalid proposals were rejected by the General Assembly of the State of Georgia and twelve other Southern States, as well as of sundry Northern States, the so-called 39th and 40th Congresses, in flagrant disregard of the United States Constitution, by the use of military force,

S.R. No. 39

dissolved the duly recognized State Governments in Georgia and nine of the other Southern States and set up military occupation or puppet state governments, which compliantly ratified the invalid proposals, thereby making (at the point of the bayonet) a mockery of Section 4, Article IV of the Constitution, guaranteeing "to every State in this Union a Republican Form of Government," and guaranteeing protection to "each of them against invasion," and

WHEREAS, further, the pretended ratification of the so-called 14th and 15th Amendments by Georgia and other States whose sovereign powers had been unlawfully seized by force of arms against the peace and dignity of the people of those States, were necessary to give color to the claim of the so-called 40th and 41st Congresses that these so-called amendments had been ratified by three-fourths of the States; and

WHEREAS, it is a well-established principle of law that the mere lapse of time does not confirm by common acquiescence an invalidly-enacted provision of law just as it does not repeal by general desuetude a provision validly enacted; and

WHEREAS, the Continued recognition of the 14th and 15th Amendments as valid parts of the Constitution of the United States is incompatible with the present day position of the United States as the World's champion of Constitutional governments resting upon the consent of the people given through their lawful representatives;

NOW, THEREFORE, BE IT RESOLVED BY THE GENERAL ASSEMBLY OF THE STATE OF GEORGIA:

The Congress of the United States is hereby memorialized and respectfully urged to declare that the exclusions of the Southern Senators and Representatives from the 39th, 40th and 41st Congresses were malignant acts of arbitrary power and rendered those Congresses invalidly constituted; that the forms of law with which those invalid Congresses attempted to clothe the submission of the 14th and 15th Amendments and to clothe the subsequent acts to compel unwilling States to ratify those invalidly proposed amendments, imparted no validity of these acts and amendments; and that the so-called 14th and 15th Amendments to the Constitution of the United States are null and void and of no effect.

BE IT FURTHER RESOLVED THAT copies of this memorial be transmitted forthwith by the Clerk of the House and the Secretary of the Senate of the State of Georgia to the President of the United States, the Chief Justice of the United States, the President of the Senate and the Speaker of the House of Representatives of Congress of the United States, and the Senators and Representatives in the Congress from the State of Georgia.

A PROPOSED AMENDMENT RELATIVE TO POWERS RESERVED FOR THE STATE[1]

July 5, 1957

MR. SIKES introduced the following joint resolution; which was referred to the Committee on the Judiciary.

JOINT RESOLUTION

Proposing an amendment to the Constitution of the United States relating to the powers reserved to the States by the tenth amendment to the Constitution.

Resolved by the Senate and House of Representatives of the United States of America in Congress assembled (two-thirds of each House concurring therein), That the following article is hereby proposed as an amendment to the Constitution of the United States which shall be valid to all intents and purposes as part of the Constitution when ratified by the legislatures of three-fourths of the several States:

ARTICLE

SECTION 1. The powers reserved to the several States by the tenth amendment to this Constitution shall be construed to include, but not be limited to, power to enact laws to promote the public peace, safety and welfare and to provide for good order, education, and harmonious race relations therein. In these enumerated fields, except where the Congress of the United States by legislation provides expressly to the contrary, the laws of each State shall govern.

SECTION 2. This article shall be inoperative unless it shall have been ratified as an amendment to the Constitution by the legislatures of three-fourths of the several States, as provided in the Constitution, within seven years from the date of its submission to the States by Congress.

A PROPOSED AMENDMENT VESTING THE SENATE WITH APPELLATE COURT FUNCTIONS[2]

July 5, 1957

MR. SIKES introduced the following joint resolution; which was referred to the Committee on the Judiciary.

JOINT RESOLUTION

Proposing an amendment to the Constitution of the United States vesting the Senate of the United States with certain appellate court functions.

Resolved by the Senate and House of Representatives of the United States of America in Congress assembled (two-thirds of each House concurring therein), That the following article is hereby proposed as an amendment to the Constitution of the United States which shall be valid to all intents and purposes as part of the Constitution when ratified by the legislatures of three-fourths of the several States:

ARTICLE

SECTION 1. The Senate of the United States shall comprise a court with final appellate jurisdiction to review decisions and judgments of the Supreme Court of the United States where questions of the powers reserved to the States, or the people, are either directly or indirectly involved and decided and a State is a party or anywise interested in such question involved and

[1] 85th Congress, 1st Session, H. J. RES. 394.

[2] 85th Congress, 1st Session, H. J. RES. 395.

decided. The Senate's exercise of such final appellate jurisdiction shall be under such rules and regulations as may be provided by the Senate, including the time within which appeals shall be taken. A decision of the Senate affirming, modifying, or reversing a decision or judgment of the Supreme Court of the United States shall be final.

SECTION 2. This article shall be inoperative unless it shall have been ratified as an amendment to the Constitution by the legislatures of three-fourths of the several States, as provided in the Constitution, within seven years from the date of its submission to the States by Congress.

EXECUTIVE ORDER AUTHORIZING USE OF FEDERAL TROOPS AT LITTLE ROCK

EXECUTIVE ORDER

PROVIDING ASSISTANCE FOR THE REMOVAL OF AN OBSTRUCTION OF JUSTICE WITHIN THE STATE OF ARKANSAS.

Whereas on Sept. 23, 1957, I issued Proclamation No. 3204 reading in part as follows:

"Whereas certain persons in the state of Arkansas, Individually and in unlawful assemblages, combinations, and conspiracies, have wilfully obstructed the enforcement of orders of the United States District Court for the Eastern District of Arkansas with respect to matters relating to enrollment and attendance at public schools, particularly at Central High School, located in Little Rock school district, Little Rock, Arkansas; and

"Whereas such wilfull obstruction of justice hinders the execution of the laws of that state and of the United States, and makes it impracticable to enforce such laws by the ordinary course of judicial proceedings; and

"Whereas such obstruction of justice constitutes a denial of the equal protection of the laws secured by the Constitution of the United States and impedes the course of justice under those laws;

"Now, therefore, I, Dwight D. Eisenhower, President of the United States, under and by virtue of the authority vested in me by the Constitution and statutes of the United States, including Chapter 15 of Title 10 of the United States Code, particularly Sections 332, 333 and 334 thereof, do command all persons engaged in such obstruction of justice to cease and desist therefrom, and to disperse forthwith"; and

Whereas the command contained in that proclamation has not been obeyed and willful obstruction of enforcement of said court orders still exists and threatens to continue:

Now, therefore, by virtue of the authority vested in me by the Constitution and statutes of the United States, including Chapter 15 of Title 10, particularly Sections 332, 333 and 334 thereof, and Section 301 of Title 3 of the United States Code, it is hereby ordered as follows:

Section 1. I hereby authorize and direct the Secretary of Defense to order into the active military service of the United States as he may deem appropriate to carry out the purposes of this order, any or all of the units of the National Guard of the United States and of the Air National Guard of the United States within the state of Arkansas to serve in the active military service of the United States for an indefinite period and until relieved by appropriate orders.

Section 2. The Secretary of Defense is authorized and directed to take all appropriate steps to enforce any orders of the United States District Court for the Eastern District of Arkansas for the removal of obstruction of justice in the state of Arkansas with respect to matters relating to enrollment and attendance at public schools in the Little Rock School District, Little Rock, Arkansas. To carry out the provisions of this section, the Secretary of Defense is authorized to use the units, and members thereof, ordered into the active military service of the United States pursuant to Section 1 of this order.

Section 3. In furtherance of the enforcement of the aforementioned orders of the United States District Court for the Eastern District of Arkansas, the Secretary of Defense is authorized to use such of the armed forces of the United States as he may deem necessary.

Section 4. The Secretary of Defense is authorized to delegate to the Secretary of the Army or the Secretary of the Air Force, or both, any of the authority conferred upon him by this order.

DWIGHT D. EISENHOWER

Suggestions for Additional Reading

Many excellent, general studies of the place of the Negro in American life are available. Among the most useful of these are: John H. Franklin, *From Slavery to Freedom* (New York, 1947); Langston Hughes, *A Pictorial History of the Negro in America* (New York, 1956); Rayford W. Logan, *The Negro in American Life and Thought* (New York, 1954); Gunnar Myrdal, *An American Dilemma* (New York, 1944); Edward F. Frazier, *The Negro in the United States* (New York, 1949); Maurice R. Davie, *Negroes in American Society* (New York, 1949); Comer V. Woodward, *The Strange Career of Jim Crow* (New York, 1955); George B. Huszar, *Equality in America* (New York, 1949).

Valuable studies dealing more specifically with race relations are: Gordon W. Allport, *Controlling Group Prejudice* (Philadelphia, 1946); Ina C. Brown, *Race Relations in a Democracy* (New York, 1949); Donald Young, *The American Negro* (Philadelphia, 1928); Earl J. Ellison, *These Rights are Ours to Keep* (New York, 1948); Naomi Goldstein, *The Roots of Prejudice Against the Negro in the United States* (Boston, 1948); Rayford W. Logan, ed., *What the Negro Wants* (Chapel Hill, 1944); Walter F. White, *How Far the Promised Land?* (New York, 1955); Helen H. Catterall, ed., *Judicial Cases Concerning American Slavery and the Negro* (Washington, 1926–1937).

The problem of segregation in its various forms has recently been the subject of a number of studies and reports. Some of the most interesting of these are: Charles S. Johnson, *Patterns of Negro Segregation* (New York, 1943); Harry S. Ashmore, *The Negro and the Schools* (Chapel Hill, 1954); Ambrose Caliver, *Education of Negro Leaders* (Washington, 1949); Eli Ginzberg, *The Negro Potential* (New York, 1956); Joseph W. Hollery, *Education and The Segregation Issue* (New York, 1955); Public Affairs Pamphlet No. 209, *Segregation and The Schools* (1954); Ira De A. Reid, ed., *Racial Desegregation and Integration* (Philadelphia, 1956); David G. Loth, *Integration North and South* (New York, 1956); Robert P. Warren, *Segregation, The Inner Conflict in the South* (New York, 1956).

Since the problem of segregation is intimately related to the 14th Amendment, such works as Horace E. Flack, *The Adoption of the 14th Amendment* (Baltimore, 1908); Joseph James, *The Framing of the Fourteenth Amendment* (Urbana, Ill., 1957); and Jacobus Ten Broek, *The Antislavery Origins of the Fourteenth Amendment* (Berkeley, Calif., 1951), should be consulted. For more specialized treatment of various aspects involved in the 14th Amendment see: Howard J. Graham, "The 'Conspiracy Theory' of the 14th Amendment" in 47 and 48 *Yale Law Journal* (1938); Charles Fairman, "Does the 14th Amendment Incorporate the Bill of Rights? The Original Understanding" 2 *Stanford Law Review* 5 (1949); Howard J. Graham, "The Early Anti-Slavery Backgrounds of the 14th Amendment," *1950 Wisconsin Law Review 479.*

Biographies of the Justices of the Supreme Court which may well be consulted are: Carl B. Swisher, *Stephen J. Field* (Washington, 1930); Carl B. Swisher, *Roger B. Taney* (New York,

1935); and F. B. Clark, *The Constitutional Doctrines of Justice Harlan* (Baltimore, 1915). For some more generalized works on the Supreme Court itself see: David M. Silver, *Lincoln's Supreme Court* (Urbana, Ill., 1956) and Charles G. Haines and Foster Sherwood, *The Role of the Supreme Court in American Government and Politics, 1835–1864* (Berkeley, Calif., 1957).

There are many recent books on the effect of the Supreme Court decision in the form of novels or symposia which give valuable insights into conditions as they exist today. Among these are: Louis D. Rubin, Jr. and James J. Kilpatrick, eds., *The Lasting South* (Chicago, 1957), wherein 14 Southerners look at their home; Omer Carmichael and Weldon James, *The Louisville Story* (New York, 1957), of how one city faced and accepted integration in its schools; and Don Shoemaker, ed., *With All Deliberate Speed* (New York, 1957), an attempt to measure objectively the degree of compliance or noncompliance with the Supreme Court's 1954 decree. Added to these, of course, are many articles available in current journals and periodicals.